Still His

Still His

One Widow's Journey to Discovery and Hope

Roni Hollis

E.L. Marker
Salt Lake City

E.L. Marker,
an imprint of WiDō Publishing
Salt Lake City, Utah
widopublishing.com

Copyright © 2017 by Roni Hollis

All rights reserved. No part of this book may be reproduced or transmitted in any form or by any means, electronic or mechanical, including photocopying, recording, or by any information storage and retrieval system without the written consent of the publisher.

Cover design by Steven Novak
Book design by Marny K. Parkin

ISBN 978-1-937178-96-3

Printed in the United States of America

For our son, Conner.
May you always hold our story
in your hands and in your heart.
MTW

If Heaven wasn't so far away . . .

Introduction

This isn't a self-help book for widows because I don't care what anyone says, nothing makes grieving a spouse, or significant other, any easier. It takes time, countless prayers, and the strongest faith in God we can muster. There is a pain so real it becomes a tangible entity inside of us, manifesting itself into a hideous monster at any given time, with no way to stop it. We can feel its heartbeat right under our own, and when it is ready to rear its ugly head and rip our soul apart once again, all we can do is breathe. Cry and breathe.

Sometimes the memories flood my mind like a torrent of despair and confusion; other times they flow from my heart like a sweet melody. Many of my memories are incredibly happy, and I will cherish those forever. I will hold them near to my heart until the day I take them to Heaven. On the flip side are the memories that break my heart and soul into pieces.

Penning them for others to read is a scary notion; I wonder how many others share similar scars. I continue to write, even when the tears are unstoppable. I will get through. I will stay strong and I will tell the stories of my scars.

I loved a man who was ripped from our world way too soon. He left behind a wife (me), two sons, and countless family and friends. Mike left this world on a cold Monday in December, in a tragic way. He was only forty-four years old.

But our story did not end on that day, nor did our love. The beginning of our story was written when I was twenty-three and he was thirty-one.

As a recent divorcée, I had not experienced the magnitude of true love until I met Mike. He became my second chance at love. We fell in love without hesitation and without end. I hope you can know the power and depth of a love unending, as I held that honor for thirteen years. I will know it again when the good Lord reunites us one day. Until that day arrives, I will hold on to my faith and to my son, our son, to see me through. On my darkest of days, I will hold on to the memories and stories that unfold before me. They are perfect and pure.

The Beginning

Chapter One

I MARRIED MY HIGH SCHOOL SWEETHEART WHEN I WAS eighteen. Our marriage lasted only five years, and then he asked for a divorce. I was twenty-three and imagined that I might live alone forever. Looking back now, the pain and struggle of my divorce is dwarfed by the pain and struggle of losing Michael.

Three months after I moved out of the house that I shared with my ex-husband, my sister Amy began teasing me about Mike Hollis. Mike had been divorced for a while from his first wife and my sister thought we would be a good fit. She would chastise me for crying constantly and would repeatedly tell me I should let her call Mike to set up a date. I brushed her off, saying Mike didn't know I existed: I was sure of it.

Since the summer I turned thirteen, my name had been synonymous with my ex-husband's. I was first his girlfriend and then his wife. The idea that anyone, especially Mike Hollis, knew me as anything other than that was ludicrous. My heart was beating to its own rhythm, convinced that a new love would never come.

I am forever grateful that my heart started beating to a new tune, and one of the first recognizable differences in that rhythm was what I thought was a chance encounter on a beautiful sunny day.

Van Buren, Missouri, is a quaint country town nestled in the heart of the Ozarks. Current River cuts a course through the middle of town, and Big Spring National Park is home to the world's largest natural spring. Our community thrives on tourism. No stoplights adorn our streets; there is no football stadium, no movie theater, not even a Wal-Mart.

In the summer months, the streets teem with out-of-state vehicles, carrying families to an outdoor adventure of hiking, canoeing, and tubing. Within our city limits is Main Street, which runs parallel to Highway 60. It is adorned on either side with the typical "Mom and Pop" restaurants, florists, antique shops, and other businesses. One such restaurant is the Jolly Cone.

As a teen I worked at the Jolly Cone, serving locals and tourists charbroiled hamburgers, jolly burgers (a homemade sloppy joe), milkshakes, and ice cream cones. The menu is filled with deep fried goodness, chili cheese nachos, and the Super Shake, a milkshake filled with cookies or sweet candies. Orders are taken at one of the red counters situated below a sliding glass window.

Metal picnic tables are spaced around the concrete patio and ceiling fans hum as customers gather to await their orders. Jolly Cone is a tradition in our little town, and Van Buren would not be the same without it. Residents hold fond feelings about this hometown staple. One of my favorite memories has Michael at the center.

One beautiful September afternoon, I was at the Jolly Cone with a friend. We were sitting at a table when Mike pulled up in an old, beat up Toyota pickup truck. He smiled at me as he walked to the order window; and as he passed by my table, he said, "Hi, how are you?"

Wow, his smile. He could light a fire within anyone with that smile. Dimples adorned his cheeks, and his slightly crooked teeth made his smile all the more endearing. Mike's smile had an orneriness to it, the kind that lingers under the surface, just daring to begin something mischievous. That was my Michael's smile. Full of endearment, fun, orneriness, honesty, playfulness, and kindness.

I smiled back and said, "Good, you?" He replied with the same.

Once he left, my friend teased me that Mike had flirted with me. I did not believe her and told her he was only being nice.

Another time, my sister and I were at Wal-Mart in the neighboring town when we ran into Mike and his four-year-old son. He shared his daddy's radiant smile and seemed to be bouncing off the walls with glee at the newly purchased Power Ranger I could see in Mike's cart.

Mike was all smiles and spoke nicely to me. We encountered each other inside the store, passing each other down one aisle and then again at the checkout register. I was too insecure to fathom Mike's desire to flirt with me, to speak with me, or to even look at me. I smiled politely and averted my eyes to the floor. Inside, my heart beat rapidly and my stomach filled with nerves. I wanted to be desired again, to be found pretty and sweet and nice. My divorce had left me devoid of confidence. But, at that point, Mike was just a friendly face and a kind smile. I never dreamed he would become so much more. I never dreamed he would become everything.

When my sister and I wheeled our cart to the parking lot, we realized that Mike's truck and my sister's vehicle were parked directly across from each other. Again, we all waved, smiled, and told each other to have a great rest of the day.

Later in our relationship, Mike told me that these encounters, which I assumed were random, had filled him with excitement. At the Jolly Cone, our meeting had not been random at all. He pretended that he needed to buy a soda that day, but that was not his real purpose; seeing my smile was. He already had a full drink in his truck, but he saw me sitting there and wanted to say hi. The Wal-Mart meeting was by chance, as was the parking across from each other, but he had sought me out inside the store.

After living with my mom for one month after my divorce, I rented a small apartment in town. When Mike learned of this, he tried his hardest to arrange more "chance" encounters. He would drive by, trying to muster the nerve to stop and ask me out. One time when my sister and I hosted a yard sale at my new apartment, Mike drove by and waved and smiled. He had planned to stop and ask me out then, but my sister's presence stopped him.

Soon after, I moved to a cheaper house outside of town. I was accustomed to living alone, to coming and going as I pleased, and to all things associated with the life of a single woman.

In August of that year, I began my teaching career. I graduated with an Elementary Education degree and took my first job as a fourth-grade teacher. I also served as a middle school assistant volleyball coach. I spent many evenings out late at a ballgame or other school function; travel time to and from the school district where I worked totaled almost two hours.

I was busy and active, and my nerves from the divorce had taken over my appetite, causing me to lose about twenty-five pounds. I was becoming a new me, surviving the divorce and thriving on my own. One day while looking in the mirror, I decided I didn't look too bad, and if someone asked me out, I would go. I even called my ex-husband to tell him this epiphany I had. Not that he cared, but it made me feel good to affirm that I would be okay without him.

Living on my own was a freedom I hadn't known before. At twenty-three, I was finally gaining my own independence. My confidence still lacked, but my determination to be okay grew each day. I began thinking that happiness was somewhere on the horizon of life; I just had to be patient.

In fact, I had no idea that my patience was not necessary: true, perfect, and pure love was just around the bend.

Chapter Two

I ARRIVED HOME FROM WORK ON THURSDAY, OCTOBER 18, 2001, when my phone rang. "You're never going to believe who just called!" said my sister Amy.

"Who?"

"Mike Hollis!" She squealed with delight like a little girl.

"Yeah, right, Amy. Don't mess with me."

"I'm not kidding! He called a few minutes ago and asked for your number. He's going to call you!"

Hesitantly I asked, "Well, what did he say?"

Mike had asked Amy what happened between my ex-husband and me, and if there was any chance of us getting back together. Amy told him no chance. The story of my divorce unfolded over their telephone conversation. Mike wondered if Amy thought I'd like to go out sometime or if I was dating anyone. My sister told him I was not dating anyone and would love to go out with him; she was sure of it.

"I'm telling you, Roni Lynn, he's going to call you!"

"Well, even if he does, it doesn't mean he'll call tonight. He may change his mind and never call me. Who knows?" Insecurities crippled me. I had never been on what I considered a "real date." The summer I turned thirteen my ex-husband and I began "going out," but we never really went anywhere until I turned fifteen. In the 1990s, "going out" often meant we passed notes between classes. There was never any actual *going* anywhere. At least not in my world.

Then we immediately became a couple so I did not consider any of those times an actual date. We had been a couple for two years before my mom allowed us to go on a date. After five years of marriage, we divorced. I was excited to feel the desire to live again, and that living began with one phone call.

Mike called me that evening, at five-forty p.m., and changed my life forever. I instantly fell in love with everything about Mike Hollis. He was so sexy; his voice raspy and perfect; his laugh, contagious. I felt the warmth in his smile and the sincerity in his words. I instantly felt safe. I laughed when he laughed and could hear the confidence in his words. His laugh felt like home on a summer day, with cold watermelon and sweet tea in the front yard while the sun warmed my skin.

We spoke for forty minutes. We discussed his marriage and divorce, my marriage and divorce, both of our jobs, our families, and finally what we each enjoyed when it came to the idea of dating. I told Mike that I was a country girl. I could dress up and go out, or I could throw on my ball cap and ride the dirt roads. We talked and laughed and planned our first date. I was excited but also skeptical. I was scared of rejection, of disappointing Mike, and of things just not working out.

Toward the end of our first phone conversation, Mike asked me to dinner on Friday. I had already made plans to visit a friend in Festus for the weekend. Mike sounded disappointed that I had plans, so I decided it was up to me to make this work.

"Well, even though I'm going out of town on Friday, I will be home Sunday." I hoped he could hear the desire to see him in my voice. I held my breath while I awaited his answer.

"Okay, well how about I cook you dinner Sunday evening?" He was smiling. I could tell.

"Sure, that sounds good."

With the end of that first phone call came hives and uncontrollable shaking. I had just been asked out on my first actual date.

At twenty-three. My first marriage was officially over. Accepting Mike's offer for dinner solidified it.

I would not let the feeling of failure prevent me from trying again. So, I allowed hope into my heart. I could not wait for Sunday to arrive.

Dinner on that first date, Sunday, October 21, was comfortable and easy. The conversation flowed. I helped him cook dinner: steak, baked potato, salad, and macaroni and cheese. He had a small bottle of every kind of salad dressing that exists, because he didn't know which kind I liked.

Apparently Mike had called my sister earlier in the day to ask what I might like to eat for dinner. According to Mike, who told me this weeks afterward, the conversation went like this:

"So, what does your sister like to eat?"

"Everything."

"Okay, what about to drink?" Mike laughed as he asked this next question.

"Grape Kool-Aid." Wow. My sister made me out to be a chunky twelve-year-old.

Luckily for me, this particular exchange did not deter Mike from going forward with our first date.

I called Mike when I returned home from my weekend in Festus. I wanted to let him know that I would be going to my sister's house to see my niece, Alyssa. Alyssa was less than one year old and was the light of my life. Alyssa kept me smiling through the tears of my divorce. We often played on the floor, giggling and wrestling. I tried to see her every single day during her first year of life, and since I had been out of town for much of the weekend, seeing her was my first priority.

"I just wanted to let you know that I made it back from Festus, but I am going to my sister's before I come out to your place."

"Okay, that's fine. I hope you had a good weekend," he replied.

"I did, thanks. So, what time do you want me out there?"

Now, this is where the Mike Hollis' smooth moves really kicked into overdrive. He responded with, "Ten minutes ago."

"Well, how about four?" I asked through a smile.

"Perfect. I'll see you then."

I called my sister for advice on what to wear. Amy suggested that I wear jeans, my Doc Martens boots that were so popular in the 1990s, and my tight red Tommy Hilfiger shirt. She said it made my chest look large. Aye aye aye, sisters. Nice. I worried that I would be too self-conscious in a tight red shirt accentuating my chest, but I went with it. What did I have to lose?

On the drive to his farm in Garwood, the one where we would later start our family, my nerves were in full swing. I was afraid of disappointing him on this first date.

But the beauty stretching out in front of me took those nerves away.

A small single-wide trailer sat atop a grassy hill; a gravel drive pulled right up to the end of the trailer, and a large barn was nestled in a grove of trees at the bottom of the hill. Green pasture rolled in front of the house, and a creek cut the fields in half. Black and red cattle grazed and bellowed as I parked my Dodge Dakota truck beside Mike's gray, tattered Toyota truck.

As I stepped from my truck and walked around the edge of the trailer, Mike peered out of the house through the sliding glass door opening. He wore a gray sleeveless Nike T-shirt, Carhartt blue jeans, and boots. His hair was dark and long enough that it parted in the middle. He smiled so big when he saw me.

"Hey, glad you found it!" he said. "I was worried you'd think you were lost."

Walking toward the house, I answered, "Ha . . . I did for a minute but I remember you telling me I'd think that and just to keep going."

Mike leaned against the open doorway and smiled. I knew right that second I was going to love him. My future stood before me.

Mike poured me a glass of grape Kool-Aid, thanks to Amy, and we began preparing dinner. My job was the macaroni and cheese. His jobs were the salad, baked potatoes, and steak. We shared small talk while we moved fluidly around the small kitchen. It seemed so natural.

During dinner, we sat on barstools in the kitchen. The conversation turned to dating.

"So, have you dated anyone since the divorce?" he said.

"Umm, no. I actually have never really dated. I mean, we were together from the summer I turned thirteen, so I've never really known what dating was like." I hesitated then said, "Can I ask what you expect of this?"

Mike looked confused. He placed his fork on his plate. I panicked, thinking I had asked the wrong question. But I had to know. I was afraid all he wanted was a physical relationship and that he would use me and lose me.

"What do you mean?" he asked.

"I mean, what do you expect? Like physically? I just want to know, because I have to tell you I have never been with anyone else besides my ex. Never. And I don't know if that's what you want or not, but I need things to go slow. Like, baby steps slow."

Mike smiled and shook his head a little as he looked at me. "Well, that is totally fine. I'm good with baby steps. I'm not looking for anything to happen right off. I thought we could have dinner and get to know each other and if we like each other, then maybe continue. But I'm not pressuring you into anything and that's fine. Baby steps it is."

Whew. I realized I had not taken a breath since I stopped speaking. Baby steps. Good call.

After dinner, Mike asked if I wanted to take a ride around his farm. We hopped in the old Toyota farm truck and rode for hours, solving all the world's problems and falling in love. I had never been so attracted to anyone in my life.

I watched his arm muscles flex each time he shifted gears. His smile sparkled. His laugh was so pure. He would toss his head back when something struck him as funny. His hazel eyes shone with the reflection of the sun setting in the distance. The road, or lack thereof, we traveled was rough and bumpy, so I had to grip the door handle. The windows were down and the wind tossed my hair everywhere, but I did not care that it looked wild and unkempt. The ride was fun.

Six hours after I arrived at Mike's farm, it was ten p.m., and I knew my alarm for school in the morning would come too soon. It was time to leave. Mike followed me to the front deck and we exchanged goodbyes. I lingered on the top step for a while, hoping for a kiss. But apparently he had taken my baby steps talk seriously.

"I'll call you tomorrow, if that's okay," Mike said, as I went down the steps.

"Yeah, I'd like that." We waved goodbye and I walked to my truck. I could not stop smiling the entire drive home.

Chapter Three

On Monday at work, everyone knew something had shifted in me. I smiled all day, thinking of Mike. Around one in the afternoon, a bouquet of beautiful flowers arrived at my classroom. I was shocked. I had not received flowers from anyone since my teens.

The card read, "Thanks for being you, Mike."

Another of the Mike Hollis smooth moves.

After I returned from school later that afternoon, I drove into Van Buren to see if, just by chance, Mike was in town. I felt like a kid trying to find her crush cruising town on a Friday night! I just had to see him.

I found him at a local convenience store, but did not pull into the parking lot. Instead, I pulled into a half-circle drive across the street. As soon as he saw me, he did the same. We met each other in our vehicles, parked window to window so we could talk.

"Hey, how was your day?" I asked.

"Good, but I kept getting made fun of," he replied through that radiant smile I already loved.

"Oh yeah? How come?"

"I haven't quit smiling all day."

The Mike Hollis smooth moves again.

"Well, that's good, I guess. Could be worse, huh? I was made fun of a little too."

"Oh yeah? About the flowers?" He laughed.

"Yeah, but they are beautiful. Thank you."

"You're welcome. So whatcha doin' now?" he asked.

"I'm going home to change. Just chill, I guess."

"Is it okay if I come over?"

"Sure," I said hesitantly. I was just so scared. I knew I already loved him, but what if I failed again? What if I could not make him happy or he did not love me back? What if I got hurt again? I forced the thoughts down and headed to my house with Mike following.

"Well, this is it. It isn't much, but I like it," I said as I began the grand tour of the two-bed, one-bath rental property.

"Yeah, it's cute," Mike said.

Before I finished showing him the garage, my sister called.

"Mike is here," I said.

Good thing Mike could not hear what "oohs" came from the opposite side of the conversation. Amy squealed with delight and then asked what Mike and I wanted to eat from McDonald's.

I warned Mike that my sister was close to certifiable over this dating thing. He just laughed and said he thought it was sweet that she was so excited about us dating. Even though we had only been on one date, my heart fluttered when he referred to us as "dating."

Not too long after my sister and her family arrived, I felt ill. Exhaustion settled into me and I felt nauseous. Sleep had evaded me since the divorce, and I was rising by five a.m., to shower and get to my school in Mountain View, thirty minutes away. Plus, I was still coaching, and when they were away games, I didn't arrive back home until midnight.

After my sister and her family left, Mike and I sat on my couch. I leaned forward with my head resting in my hands. He pulled me closer to him so that my head rested on his right shoulder.

I heard his heart beating. It felt so safe and warm, like where I belonged. We sat in silence for a few minutes.

"I'm sorry you don't feel well," he said.

"Me too." I tilted my head up and Mike kissed me on top of my head. I looked up a little more and he kissed me on the forehead.

Butterflies overtook the nausea in my stomach. My hands shook. My heart fluttered.

I looked up once more and Mike kissed me on the lips. A gentle, perfect, soft and meaningful kiss. I melted. All the sadness, the sorrow, and the feelings of defeat disappeared. In one instant, in one unspoiled moment, my world changed.

Mike left soon after that first kiss. He traveled four hours from Van Buren to Columbia, for his Missouri Rural Water job. Mike offered technical assistance to water and wastewater treatment plants, and he also taught certification courses required for licensing an operator of water and wastewater plants. He usually traveled a few days a week, requiring overnight stays.

On Tuesday, Wednesday, and Thursday, we talked on the phone into the wee hours of the morning. I am unsure how we managed to stay up so late, until at least two or three a.m., and then work the following days. During Thursday's conversation, Mike asked me a question that set our entire future into motion.

"So, how do you feel about us?"

I was unsure how to respond. I decided to play it cool. "Good, I guess. What about you?" That was it; turn the tables and make him say it first.

"Well," he began, and my heart pounded so loudly I thought he could hear it through the phone, "I was not looking for anything. I know neither of us were. And I know this sounds crazy, but I just have to tell you. I'm falling in love with you."

"Hallelujah!" and "Praise Jesus!" is what I wanted to yell into the receiver. But I didn't. "Hmm . . . good," I breathed. "I am falling in love with you, too, but I was afraid to say it first. I thought you'd think I was crazy!"

"Haha, nope, I don't think you're crazy. I mean, maybe a little to fall in love with me, but still . . . you're not crazy. You're actually more than I could ever imagine. And I can't believe how this past week, and most of our phone conversations, have made such a difference in me."

I listened with tears streaming down my face.

"I mean, I never expected this, you know? I thought we'd have a good time, see each other a few times, and maybe that would be it. Especially after your baby steps talk!" he laughed.

"I never imagined this happening either, Mike. Seriously. I was scared to death to go on a date with you. I was scared you'd want more than I was willing to give, scared I would give more than I should, scared you'd not be happy with me, that I wasn't pretty enough, smart enough, or any of it. I was just scared." I paused. "But, I'm not anymore. You don't scare me. You make me want to be happy."

"You make me want to be happy, too."

And that was it. We both fell hard and fast. From October 18, 2001, for thirteen years, not a single day passed when we didn't see or speak to each other multiple times a day.

When we first fell in love, I noticed Mike's golden smile and his hazel eyes that twinkled when he looked at me. And when Mike looked at me, he really looked *at me*. His gaze seemed to go all the way through to my soul and know my deepest desires, my most secret fears, and my purest dreams.

His hands were rough and worn from years of work, and his skin always sun-kissed. His voice was soft when he was happy and rough when he was angry.

We learned a lot about each other in a few short months. Very early on, we knew we were in it for the long haul. Mike asked me to move in with him, but for months I refused. I wanted to spend more time learning about each other. I wanted Mike to be one thousand percent sure about us, because he had a son involved.

So, for a few months we just loved each other. We went on dates and occasionally spent the night at each other's house. Since he traveled weekly, we talked for countless hours on the phone. We called each other "babe" and fell more in love each day. Mike introduced me to his son, but we were careful to limit our contact in front of him.

I prayed that Mike was the man I would spend the rest of my life with. Although I wanted marriage before living together, I caved to Mike's request. In February of 2002, I finally moved in with Mike. We decided since we had been through failed marriages and there was a little boy involved, that we needed to make sure we could stand each other on a daily basis.

And there were rough times; very rough times that scared me.

Times Mike drank too much.

Times he scared me with his temper.

Times when Mike would shut me out and I would feel so hurt.

Times I thought money really was the root of all evil and that fights over it would end us.

Times his jealousy would take control and cause him to say hurtful and hateful things to me.

With each difficult time we experienced, a million more amazingly beautiful times caught my breath and promised that God's plan was coming together for us.

Times when we couldn't even make it in the house before we fell into each other, wrapped up in love so passionately.

Times when he held me so close that I had never felt safer in my life.

Times when he looked into my eyes and went all the way through to my soul.

Times when we laughed so hard, and danced so closely, and chased each other through the house.

Times when we had heart-to-heart conversations about our future.

Times when we made plans for our life together.

Times when we worked together out on the farm, him teaching me all the way.

Times when we sat in silence, gazing at the stars, dreaming of becoming parents together one day.

Times when we went away together and enjoyed each other's company while out at dinner, at one of his work conferences, or hanging out with friends.

Times when we whispered fears to each other that no one had ever heard.

Times when we cried to each other about our fears and we wiped away each other's tears with a gentle touch.

Times when we realized we were made for each other and that is why we would fight so hard one minute and love even harder the next.

We lived together two years. We often discussed having a child of our own. I wanted to become a wife and a mom more than anything.

Being a stepmom was taxing, and it almost caused Mike and me to end our relationship before we married. Although a stepchild myself, I never appreciated everything my stepparents had been through until I experienced it. I never treated my stepparents with disrespect; however, I did want to see my parents together, without a "substitute" or "replacement." It took me years to realize that my stepparents never tried to be a replacement or substitute; they were simply another person to love and care for me. But as a girl, I struggled with that concept, and I imagine that every stepchild has as well.

A stepchild is in such a difficult position, afraid to love the stepparent too much for fear of hurting the biological parent. New boundaries are formed. Seeing a parent with someone who is essentially a stranger brings jealousies and fears, and sometimes anger and resentment moves in. I worked hard to never let that happen and to carefully tread within my stepmom boundaries. But still, something was missing. Our family was not complete.

I wanted to feel like a "real" parent and to be loved unconditionally. I wanted a child more than anything.

Chapter Four

Early in Mike's and my relationship, I had some health issues that I feared would prevent us from having a baby of our own. I experienced internal pains about a year into our relationship and decided to see the doctor. I scheduled an appointment for a routine checkup, thinking maybe I had a urinary tract infection, or maybe a cyst on my ovaries.

Instead of the usual checkup, I came home to the farm sore from an ovarian biopsy. Mike was at the barn under the small grove of trees, working on a tractor. He could tell I was upset by the look on my face.

"What's up, babe?" he asked.

"I guess it isn't just a UTI or a cyst. I don't know what it is, but she took a chunk from my ovary to biopsy it."

"What? What the heck is it?" His expression showed worry.

"I don't know, babe, but what if something is really wrong? What if I have cancer or something and we can't have kids?" I cried with every word. I felt like my worst fear was coming to fruition.

Mike held me close. He held on to me tightly and whispered into my ear that everything was going to be all right. I wasn't so sure.

"But what if it's not? What if I can't have kids and you won't want me anymore." Stupid thought, yes, but that is where my mind went.

"Babe, it's going to be okay. And if that happens, which it won't, we'll deal with it then. okay?" Mike grabbed my shoulders and tilted my tear-stained face to meet his gaze. "And, I'm not going anywhere, whether you can have kids or not."

I saw him cry for the first time. He really did love me. And no matter what, we were going to fight through this together. Fortunately, within a few months of some in-office procedures, like cervical scraping and freezing, my doctor took care of the pre-cancer cells and things returned to normal.

Within another year my fears were assuaged. We would have no problem conceiving.

I wanted to be married before we had a child. In the summer of 2003, we planned for an August wedding. But Mike still had not purchased an engagement ring.

That summer I traveled with Mike for his Missouri Rural Water job. I packed books to read, usually Nicholas Sparks or John Grisham, and my CD case. When Mike stopped at a treatment plant, I sat in the truck and read or listened to music.

In June we traveled to Branson West, about four hours from home. I asked Mike if we could stop in Springfield to look at Zales rings. We had just enough time to peruse Zales' ring selection before traveling another forty minutes to Branson West, where Mike needed to conduct a smoke test to determine leaks in the water pipes. As we looked at the rings, I could not decide. I wanted them all!

But Mike was determined that he was going to get it right, and that meant I had to at least give him three options from which to choose. Easy.

I would have been happy with anything. "Babe, seriously, you could give me a bread wrapper and I'd marry you! I don't care which one, just get me one!"

I selected three of my favorite wedding sets and soon we left for Branson West. After hours of smoke testing, Mike walked back to the truck. He looked exhausted. I knew we were not going back to Springfield to purchase a ring. My heart sank.

"Sorry, babe, I'm just worn out," he said.

The spoiled brat in me said, "Fine. Let's go home."

I dozed against the glass of the passenger door and did not know until I opened my eyes that we were parked in the Battlefield Mall parking lot in Springfield. Joy returned to my soul!

"Don't get too excited; you're staying in here," Mike said.

"Okay, I'll stay!" I clapped my hands together.

"I'll be back in a few minutes." He exited the truck while I bounced up and down in my seat.

Twenty minutes passed and my cell phone rang. Mike said, "You could go into JC Penney and look for shoes, but remember, they need to be flats. I don't want you taller than me in our wedding pictures."

I happily agreed, locked the door, and entered JC Penney. I wandered straight to the shoe department and found a pair of ivory flats I liked. I was about to ask a salesperson to get my size when my cell phone rang again.

"Babe, do you have the keys?" Mike asked in an exasperated voice. I heard car alarms in the background.

"Well, yes, you told me to come inside and I always lock the truck. What's going on?"

"I need you to come out here and unlock it. I tried to get in and set the alarm off."

I rushed from the store and jogged to the truck, pressing the panic button on the key fob. Mike sat in the driver's seat, his chin resting on his hand, when I climbed into the seat. I looked around; no Zales bag in sight. Mike was drenched in sweat.

"How did you get in?" I asked, my eyes still scanning the interior of the truck.

"I climbed in the back glass. That's why the alarm went off." He started the truck as he answered.

"Oh, okay, well, sorry. You told me to go, so I figured you wanted me to lock the door." I scanned the front seat, the floor board, and the back seat. "So, how did it go?" I finally asked.

"I couldn't do it," he said calmly, as he navigated the mall's parking lot.

Irritation and panic took over. "What do you mean you couldn't do it?"

"Babe, calm down, I just couldn't do it, okay?"

First, no man should ever tell a woman to calm down. That solves nothing and it only increases the anxiety. Second, he couldn't do it? The wedding date was set. The venue was booked. The dress was in my mom's closet. In two months we were to be married. What in the world did he mean by telling me he couldn't do it? Hot tears poured from my eyes. I was reliving my old relationship.

Two months before my ex-husband and I married, he broke it off. I got off work late one night and went to the small trailer his mom had purchased for us. My ex-husband had wanted to call off the wedding at that point, but then he called me the following morning. Two months later we went forward with our wedding, only for the marriage to end in five short years.

Now the same thing was happening, an omen I could not accept.

"Oh my gosh! What do you mean you couldn't do it? Do you mean you can't marry me? Or that you just couldn't do it right now? Like what? We have everything set! If you're calling it off, then *you* will tell everyone! I cannot believe this is happening again! What is wrong with me?" I was full on wailing now, not from anger, but from hurt. I was heartbroken. I was devastated and sure that Mike Hollis was done with me altogether.

And I was not going to be the one to call Hidden Acres Wedding Chapel in Eureka Springs, Arkansas. Mike would have to call them after he broke the news to his family.

"Oh my gosh, you are such a baby! Look!" Mike lifted the lid of the console between us.

Inside the dirty and cluttered console was a beautiful white Zales bag. Mike slammed the console lid closed and said, "There, you brat! There it is!"

"Babe!" I wiped tears from my hot face.

"What?" he yelled back.

"I'm sorry. I thought you were breaking up with me. You can't say that kind of stuff to me and not think I'm going to get upset. I'm sorry, can I see it, please?" I held my clasped hands under my chin, ready to beg if necessary.

"No, you can't have it. You're a spoiled brat and I can't believe you cried and freaked out."

"Well, Michael Richard Hollis, you tell the woman you're supposed to marry that you couldn't buy her a ring and that you panicked in the jewelry store, and then she can't be upset? I said I'm sorry, but you hurt my feelings! I thought you were breaking up with me and didn't want to get married two months before our already scheduled wedding! Please, can I see it?"

He said, "Well, I want to wait until sometime romantic on the farm or something, so you're not getting it yet."

"This *is* romantic." We were traveling seventy miles per hour on the highway.

"Ugh, fine." He opened the console and pulled out the white bag. "Here." He shoved the bag in my direction.

"No. You have to ask me."

"Oh my gosh, you're getting on my nerves. It's a good thing I love you," he said as he pulled into a roadside park. Diesels and family vehicles filled the parking lot. Families loitered around the playground. Travelers waited in line at the bathroom and at the vending machines.

Mike parked the truck but kept the engine running for the air conditioning. It was a sweltering June day. I was giddy. I held my hands clasped together in excitement and anticipation.

Mike opened the Zales bag and pulled a gray velvet box from within. He opened the lid and before me sat my favorite of the three choices I had given him earlier in the day. A large marquise cut diamond engagement ring nestled among a wedding band. The band was adorned with matching smaller marquise cut diamonds and three small baguette diamonds along the edge. It sparkled and shone.

I gasped. "Oh my gosh, baby, it's beautiful! It's my favorite one!"

"Well?" he asked.

"Well, say it please."

"You are ridiculous."

I smiled. "But you love me. And please, I just want to hear you say it."

"Fine. Will you marry me?"

"*Yes!*" I screamed and wrapped my arms around his neck, almost crawling over the console to reach him. I kissed him over and over before I retreated to my seat. "Can you put it on me?"

Mike slid the engagement ring onto my finger. My dream came true. The rest of the drive home I alternately stared at my finger and called all the important people in our families. Everyone knew we were getting married in two months, but they were awaiting the ring, just like me.

The two months before our wedding passed quickly. Mike would not allow any family to attend. I wanted our immediate family members there, but he wanted it to be just us. Part of his reasoning was that we both had failed marriages that began with large weddings and he did not want another "huge production." We argued about it a few times until I consented. It would be very intimate. And the venue would record it for us, so the family could watch at a dinner we would hold upon our return home.

The wedding weekend arrived. Mike planned to take off work early in the afternoon to shower and rest before the four hour drive to Eureka Springs. I packed for us early in the day, cleaned the house, and collected my dress from my mom's house, completely ready by one p.m. The clock struck six before Michael arrived home. I was so angry. It was another one of the countless times work came before family. But I am a patient woman. Or at least I was then.

Our first night in Eureka Springs was spent in near silence. Mike felt angry that I was aggravated at him for not leaving work earlier in the day. I felt aggravated that he had not followed through on his promise to leave work early.

We checked into our small cabin and ventured into town for dinner, a very late dinner. We found a quaint restaurant where our moods lightened with food and beer. After dinner we returned to our cabin and, almost immediately, fell fast asleep.

Our wedding day arrived with sunshine and a breeze. We met with the owners of the Hidden Acres Wedding Chapel, who also owned the small cabin in which we stayed. They were a husband and wife team; the wife performing the ceremony and the husband as photographer. They provided a small cake, champagne, music, and fresh flowers. After reviewing the details of the ceremony taking place later that evening, Mike and I headed to the county courthouse to purchase our wedding license.

In Missouri at the time, wedding licenses had to be purchased at least three days prior to the wedding ceremony. In Arkansas, they could be purchased on the same day as the wedding. Mike joked that he wondered if we were even legally married since we did not have to wait for the license.

We stood in line behind an older couple, maybe in their midsixties, eagerly awaiting our turn. Mike's face did not hide his skepticism of the whole same-day purchase.

We completed the necessary paperwork and before we were finished, the older couple returned, already married. I could see the wheels turning inside Mike's mind: he wanted to run down the street to wherever this couple had gone and get married, skipping the entire ceremony.

"Babe—" he started.

"No. We are getting married *tonight* with a dress and roses and everything!"

The newlyweds laughed. Mike laughed, too, and just shrugged his shoulders and said, "All right. Didn't figure you'd let me but thought I'd try."

We purchased our license and roamed town until we found a quaint café for breakfast. The café décor exuded the 1950's era. Black-and-white-checkered tiles covered the floor, wait staff wore pink dresses with white aprons, Formica tables adorned the dining area, and a large jukebox filled one corner. We sat among an older generation of visitors. I imagined the café must be the morning "watering hole" that many small towns have, where the men sit and drink their morning coffee and gossip, and the ladies discuss their current quilt pattern.

After breakfast, we returned to the cabin. The cabin was one large room with an adjoining bathroom. A small kitchenette, dining table, TV, faux fireplace, and queen-sized bed filled the main room. A hot tub sat beside a BBQ grill on a wooden porch.

"Wanna watch a movie?" Mike asked.

We perused the old VHS cassette tapes and settled on *Lethal Weapon 2*. Shortly after it began, Mike and I fell asleep. We awoke to the sound of Mike's phone alarm set for my hair appointment. We lay on the bed, facing each other.

"We're getting married today," Mike whispered.

I smiled. "I know. Are you happy?"

"Yes, I am. Are you?" He reached his hand over to hold mine.

"Yes. I hope we are always happy, you know? I'm sorry I was upset last night when you got home late. I didn't mean to be hateful. I just wanted to get here. To spend time with you here."

He released my hand and caressed my right cheek. I felt the hard callouses on his hand, but also the softness of his touch. In a few short hours I would marry my best friend. I had a second chance at love, at happiness, at a family, and at forever. Tears welled in my eyes. It was really happening. I was in love with a man who loved me in return, and we were about to build a life together, a life made of our dreams.

"I love you. And I hope we're always happy, too." Mike leaned in and kissed me slowly and gently. He wiped away my tears and kissed the tip of my nose. "But, you better get going for your hair appointment or you're gonna be late."

I rose from the bed, gathered my purse and drove toward town, following directions provided by the owners of Hidden Acres.

I returned to the cabin two hours later. Mike said he was hungry, so he left me to apply my makeup and went to find us something to eat for a late lunch.

At three, my future husband and I shared a Subway sandwich on the queen-sized bed and finished *Lethal Weapon 2*.

It was time to dress for our wedding ceremony. I dressed first in my beautiful white lingerie and then in my ninety-nine dollar David's Bridal gown, which I had purchased months before we decided to get married.

While bridesmaid dress shopping for my cousin Jamie's wedding, I stumbled upon a beautiful gown on the sale rack. The white fabric created a perfect gown; pearls and lace filled the off-the-shoulder bodice. It fit me perfectly, requiring no alterations. My aunt and cousins supported my impulsive decision to buy a wedding dress before Mike and I were even engaged. Good thing it worked out.

Mike dressed in the main room while I dressed in the bathroom. Butterflies fluttered again; I was about to see my soon-to-be husband in his suit and tie, ready to marry me. I asked Mike if he was ready for me to come out of the bathroom.

I emerged, and my future stood with his hands folded in front of him. A black suit, white dress shirt, and silver tie dressed this handsome man. His eyes smiled before his lips did when he looked at me. His dark hair was beginning to show signs of age, with the sprinkles of gray against his temples. His facial hair was a perfectly trimmed goatee.

"Is it okay?" I asked as I stepped slowly forward.

"It's perfect, baby. You look beautiful." He held my hands. "Don't cry or you're gonna mess up your makeup." Mike wiped my tears. "You ready to get married?"

I nodded. We held hands as we left the small cabin. The August evening sun was slowly making its descent. Birds chirped in the distance and a breeze tickled our cheeks. We slowly walked toward a gazebo where a small-framed woman awaited us. Her husband, a large man, stood to the side with his camera in hand.

At seven p.m., on Saturday, August 9, 2003, I became Mrs. Mike Hollis. My heart overflowed. Our entire lives stood before us, ready for our journey as husband and wife to begin.

Chapter Five

THE JUNE BEFORE OUR WEDDING, WE DECIDED TO BEGIN our attempt at pregnancy. Mike and I took a leisurely drive to his cousin's farm, which later became our farm; and while driving the gravel road, Mike asked if I wanted to wait a while to start trying to get pregnant, or if I wanted to start now.

"I thought we decided we would be married two years before we started trying?"

"I know," he said, "but, I figured you really didn't want to wait. If you want to start, we can."

"If you're serious, then *yes*!" I leaned over and kissed him on the cheek.

I tracked my cycle immediately, researched peak ovulation days, purchased ovulation detection kits, and prayed. July came and went with no pregnancy. August came and went with our wedding but no pregnancy. September brought the same.

With only a few months into the process, I already felt disappointment and defeat. Fear from my earlier health scare with the biopsy and treatment for pre-cancer cells created doubt. I questioned if I would even be able to have children.

October came, and I realized I was three days late.

I wanted so badly to be pregnant, to become a mom. I could not wait to take a test. Since Van Buren does not have a Wal-Mart, I purchased four Dollar General brand pregnancy tests. I used them two days in a row but could not see a second line, indicative of a positive result.

One evening I took yet another test and asked Mike to look at the line. Did he see a second pink line, barely? I thought I could, but worried it might just be me wanting it so badly I imagined the second line.

Mike looked at the stick and said, "Well, I think it's there, babe, but if you buy a Dollar General test, you'll get a Dollar General result. So, why don't you go get a real, name-brand test in the morning?"

The following morning I rose extra early and drove forty-five miles to purchase a Clearblue Easy Digital test. I considered taking the test in Wal-Mart but wanted to be with my husband when I knew the answer. Plus, that would be too much like a country song. Peeing on a pregnancy test in the Wal-Mart bathroom did not fit my plan for motherhood.

Later that day, I met Mike at my stepson's soccer game. "Well, did you take it?" Mike asked.

"No, I wanted to wait and do it with you."

He smiled. "I figured you wouldn't be able to wait."

We sat and watched the excitement of seven-year-olds playing soccer. We did not discuss the test, as we did not want anyone knowing anything until the pregnancy was confirmed.

At the time, we owned a small rental house in city limits, currently uninhabited. We decided to go there to complete the test. I went into the bathroom while Mike read the instructions out loud.

"Unwrap the test stick from the plastic. Remove the end cap from the urine strip. Hold the urine strip . . ."

"Babe, I know all that! Just get to the part that says what to do after I've peed on it."

Mike skipped forward a few steps in the manual. "So, then okay, the word—" He couldn't complete his sentence, because the word PREGNANT appeared on the tiny screen. I screamed with excitement and jumped into Mike's arms. We hugged and kissed, and of course, I cried.

My handsome husband smiled ear to ear and said, "I told you it would happen, baby. I told you! I'm glad you're happy."

"I can't believe I'm gonna be a mommy!" I kissed him and wrapped my arms tighter around his neck. He squeezed me tight and pushed me back just enough to place his hand on my lower stomach. My world was what I had always imagined it would be. I was a wife, a stepmom, and a soon to be mommy. My heart burst with happiness.

Our doctor's appointment confirmed we had conceived one week after our August wedding. It was God blessing us with perfect timing.

My pregnancy also was perfect. No morning sickness, no heartburn, no major concerns occurred. My stomach grew to massive proportions, but my husband complimented me every single day. I was in pure bliss.

One evening while Mike was out of town for his Missouri Rural Water job, I just finished with a hot bath when I experienced my first pregnancy mood swing. I dried myself and looked in the mirror at my ever-growing belly. I had carefully applied Vitamin E oil to my stomach daily for the entire seven months of my pregnancy.

"What the heck?" I yelled. My stomach was too large to see the underside, but in the mirror I saw a blue line on the lower right side. At first, I thought it was a blue vein. I retrieved my cell phone from the bedroom and took a picture. I looked closely at the picture and then ran my finger across the blue line on my stomach. There was texture to this blue line. It was no vein. It was a stretch mark. My phone rang.

"Hey babe." Mike's voice came through my sobs.

"Hi," I wailed into the phone.

"What's wrong? Are you okay? Is the baby okay?" I sensed panic in his voice.

"Yes," I cried, "we're fine, but I . . . I found my first stretch mark!" I stood naked in the bathroom, cell phone in hand, sobbing at my reflection cursed with my first stretchmark. I grabbed the Vitamin E bottle from the bathroom shelf and threw it in the trash.

"Babe, my gosh, who cares? You scared the hell outta me! You're fine with a stupid stretchmark!"

"No, I'm not. If I have one, I'll have more and be huge and gross and you're not gonna want me anymore," I said through broken sobs.

"Babe, seriously. I'll want you no matter what. I'll want you when you can't walk anymore, when your hair is gray and your teeth are missing. I'm gonna love you and want you when you have to push me around in my wheelchair. I'm gonna want you no matter if you have stretchmarks head to toe."

I calmed down with each claim of his unending desire for me.

"You're carrying our miracle baby, remember? You're beautiful and I don't care if you have stretchmarks. Be happy, baby, it's just a stretchmark."

I breathed a sigh of relief. My husband would want me and love me no matter what, until the end of time.

The remainder of my pregnancy passed smoothly and we were blessed with our angel boy, Conner. He was tiny and perfect in every way. Mike stood by my head during labor and encouraged me the entire time with, "Push, baby, push!"

I held our son in my arms and the first words I spoke to him were, "I have waited so long for you. I love you, little man." I had three men in my life who I loved endlessly. We were a family. We were whole.

Chapter Six

OUR THIRTEEN YEARS TOGETHER FLEW BY.
We were married for eleven years, four months, and twenty days when Mike was taken from us.

Mike had recently established a private contracting company in the hopes he could resign from his traveling job with Missouri Rural Water Association (MRWA). Mike enjoyed the job but hated the travel and nights away from home.

I was not keen on the idea of purchasing the concrete business, but his dream was to be self-employed, which would allow him to be home every night. I supported him in all of his business endeavors, although reluctantly. I wanted him to be happy.

With our cattle farm and other properties, Mike wanted to be more present, available to see to the full operation. Mike's step-dad, Gayle, was aging and no longer able to fulfill all the duties of operating a huge cattle farm. So, when the opportunity arose to buy a small concrete plant twenty miles from our home, he did.

We fought about it and one night he asked me, "Basically, I need to know if I do this, will you still be here?"

My husband was a workaholic. Or better put, a workaholic in overdrive. Mike never stopped working. He rarely slept. He didn't eat properly or take care of his health. He always had some plan for a new business venture, and he always purchased more and more in hopes of paying off his debt and making a profit. Had this been able to happen, he would have seen our boys more often and eventually been able to leave them a profitable farm.

Mike could never stop or slow down because he had so many obligations. Had he not been taken from us, he would have had every inch of land, every piece of equipment, and every business venture paid for in full before the age of sixty. He would have been able to give his boys what he had always dreamed of. I struggled with each new purchase or new business idea because I wanted my husband home. I missed him. I hated that we rarely had date nights, or that his family was usually in bed before Mike arrived home.

The financial strain also made me apprehensive. I worried he was getting in over his head, and that one day the overload of debt and work would kill him.

Unfortunately, I was right.

One part of his private contracting company involved mixing, delivering, and pouring concrete. One normal day, he left for work and never returned. I am blessed and grateful that on the morning of his passing we told each other we loved each other three times. But I will never fully come to terms with what happened.

On December 29, 2014, I awoke at six a.m. to the sounds of Mike's coffee pot brewing. I entered the kitchen quietly. He stood at the sink with his back resting against it and welcomed me into his arms like he did every day. I folded my hands into my chest and curled into him like a baby. He held me, kissed the top of my head, and said in his husky voice, "Hey, beautiful. I love you."

I replied, "I love you too, baby."

We talked briefly about the day's work ahead, which included a couple of small concrete jobs to deliver. I poured myself a cup of coffee and went into the playroom adjacent to the kitchen. Mike sat at the kitchen table, and I sat on the couch.

"Whatcha gonna get up to today, babe?" Mike asked.

"I think I'm going to clean the utility room out, finish putting Christmas away, and do laundry."

"Sounds good," he said.

We continued talking for a little longer, but Mike seemed unusually quiet. He sat at the table looking out our sliding glass door, as though in deep reflection. He seemed tired and almost defeated.

The night before he had slept across from Conner's room for what they called a "special night." Special nights were a tradition in our family.

Mike would either make a pallet of blankets on the floor to sleep beside one or both of his boys, or he would sleep in the bed with them, or the bed right across from them. I never minded. It helped build the relationship Mike wanted with his sons, and it reinforced his love for them. He and the boys loved their special nights. Conner had been so excited for a special night since it was a Sunday, normally not used for special nights because of school the next day. But since we were on Christmas break, it was allowed.

I assumed that Mike hadn't rested well and felt tired. I wish I had begged him to stay home. He wouldn't have, but I still wish I had tried.

After about thirty minutes he rose and said, "Well, I guess I'm not getting anything done here, am I?"

"Please be careful today, babe. I love you."

He returned the "I love you," and added, "I'll be careful."

About an hour after Mike left, Conner awoke hungry. I made cinnamon rolls and decided to call Mike to see if he was still on the farm and would like to come by and grab a couple. He answered his phone but was already out of town, between Winona and Birch Tree, the town where the concrete plant is located.

We said, "I love you" again at the end of the phone conversation. Three times that morning.

I busied myself with cleaning our utility room. It had been a mess for months, and I couldn't stand it anymore. The cow manure and dirt smells from Mike's farm and work clothes permeated the utility room.

Proud of my accomplishment, I cleaned the rest of the house before lunch. I had not even changed from my pajamas. Conner played with his Matchbox cars. Music played in the background. We were both oblivious to the reality about to crash around us.

A little before one p.m. I received a text that read: **We heard Mike got hurt today. Can you let us know what is going on and how Mike is doing when you get a chance? Thanks, hope all is okay.**

Immediately my stomach churned. My heart rate increased. My hands shook. I looked at my son quietly playing and decided to step outside to avoid him hearing the conversation.

I called Mike's phone. Never in a million years would I have imagined what I heard.

A man's voice answered and sounded breathless. I thought it was Mike. "Babe, are you okay?" I asked.

"Hello? Is this Veronica?"

I still thought it was Mike's voice. "Yes, it's me," I said. "Are you okay?" And then my world fell apart with a few simple words.

"Ma'am, I'm sorry to tell you this over the phone, but Mike has passed away."

Deafening silence. I could not breathe. The world spun around me. A million thoughts flashed in a second and everything went dark and cold. One hand went to my stomach; my cell phone shook in my other trembling hand. I couldn't believe what I just heard.

I shakily responded, "No. No, you have the wrong person. No."

"Ma'am, I'm the Shannon County coroner. I'm so sorry, but Mike had an accident at the concrete plant and he passed away."

I kept saying "No," over and over. I finally said, "Well, someone needs to come get me right now because I need to see him. Because I don't believe you. My husband is not dead and you have the wrong number."

It did not register for me that *I* had dialed Mike's number, and this man who I had never met had answered my husband's phone.

I kept verbally chastising him, telling him he had contacted the wrong person.

He told me the local law enforcement should be on their way to my house. No part of the conversation, or the fact that I stood dazed beside my truck, cell phone in hand, nausea running thick, seemed real. I felt disoriented. I hit the end button and stayed in the gravel drive for a minute, trying to collect my thoughts. Confusion settled into my brain.

As calmly as I could, I entered our house, shaking like a leaf, still in disbelief. I didn't cry. My body and mind were in shock. I did not know it then, but I do now. Shock limits our ability to comprehend things, whether actions or speech. At this point, I didn't believe any of the words just spoken to me. Mike had suffered an injury; he broke a bone; he broke his neck or back and was being airlifted to a hospital. That was my reality. That was my fear. Not that his body was a shell to the man I had loved for thirteen years; not that he was gone.

"Conner, I need you to get dressed. I don't know what's happened, but I think Daddy got hurt today and we need to go see what's going on. We shouldn't panic, but no matter what, we need to pray to God for strength. Okay?" My voice shook, but I maintained an eerie calmness while talking to Conner. What choice did I have? This was not true. Mike was *not* dead.

My little boy looked at me in shock. We both quickly dressed. My mind was not thinking clearly. A frown formed on my brow while confusion settled within me. I had a plan: we would drive to the plant to see Michael lying on a gurney, being loaded into a helicopter. We would arrive to see people loading him, moving concrete equipment and vehicles out of the helicopter's way. We would hold his hand, tell him we loved him, and follow the helicopter to the hospital. We would struggle financially with taking care of hospital bills and such, but we would be fine. That was my reality. That was my plan.

But I soon learned that my plan accounted for nothing.

Conner and I rushed to the truck and drove to the highway—our mission to reach the concrete plant in Birch Tree. Once I reached the highway, I realized I had better stay put. The fog began to lift, and I was aware enough to realize I was in no condition to drive. And, if I arrived at the concrete plant and Mike truly was dead, it would be awful for Conner.

I took a few deep breaths, we turned around, and as I pulled into our driveway, I made Conner go inside. "Son, go in for a minute. Momma's gonna make a few more phone calls to see if she can figure out what's going on. You stay in there and keep quiet, okay? Keep praying, too."

I called my stepson's mom first and explained that if I had heard correctly over the phone, Mike was dead. I told her I did not know how to tell my own son that his dad was dead. I explained that she needed to come to our house. I hung up and calls began coming in quicker than I could answer.

Of my family, my dad was the first to call. I told him I thought it was true, but I wasn't one hundred percent sure. I was hell-bent that the news of Mike's death was not reality. I told Dad I was going to call Mike's phone again because there no way was this true. Dad said he loved me and that he was driving to our home.

Mike's mom, Chris, was my next call. I explained that something was wrong; I lied and said I did not know for sure how bad, but that Mike had had an accident. I could not tell her over the phone what I had learned. Chris's heart had been broken too many times over her lifetime. She was a widow herself; Mike's dad, Bob, passed when Mike was twenty. Mike was Chris's first child; but he was her baby boy and always would be. I would not tell her over a telephone call that her firstborn son was dead.

I asked her to come to our home until we could discover what happened. She and Mike's stepdad, Gayle, lived only five minutes from us. I ended our conversation, still standing in the gravel beside my truck.

I could not accept the tragic loss of my husband, the love of my life. Once again, I dialed Mike's number. Conner had snuck outside to stand at the edge of the house while I dialed. Since my back was turned to him, I didn't know he was there.

"Are you sure?" I asked, shaking uncontrollably.

"Ma'am, he got caught and fell into the concrete truck. I'm so sorry. Is there someone I can call?"

"No!" My screams and tears finally broke free. I could not catch my breath. My insides burned, my stomach churned, my ears rang, my heart screamed. Darkness washed over me. Conner told me later that I hit my truck and fell to the ground on my knees while I screamed, "No! This can't be real! This can't be happening!"

Still completely unaware of Conner's presence beside me, I screamed and sobbed. I told the Shannon County coroner, who had twice answered my dead husband's phone, to call Erik, the funeral director in our town and one of Mike's good friends.

The sharp gravel bruising my knees did not even phase me. I rested one hand on the front driver tire and bowed my head, praying silently for God not to have done this to us. I was so angry with God at this point, when only moments earlier I had reminded my son to plead with Him for strength and to not have one measure of blame or anger toward Him.

My mind kept flashing to my husband's face and his golden smile. My breaths were sporadic. I'm unsure how the coroner even understood my words. My hands trembled, my entire body trembled. I felt cold. I was deaf to everything around me. I screamed over the phone, "*No!*" over and over. I told the coroner that the police still hadn't arrived and that he had better call someone to get here quick.

From my peripheral vision, I noticed the innocence and happiness of my beautiful son. The little boy for whom I had prayed countless prayers stood before me, unaware that his world had just shattered.

I quickly ended the phone call and bowed my head. How? How could I muster the strength to speak the words that would kill my son's happiness? I prayed to God to help me bring the words to fruition.

Conner was crying and snot poured from his nose. I looked at him and, through broken sobs and my own tears, I said, "Conner, your daddy's gone. He's gone, Conner. I'm so sorry." Those were the most difficult and worst words I have ever said to my son.

I watched my little boy crumble to the ground beside me and scream over and over my same sentiments . . . "No!" Conner, who was this rough and tough ten-year-old, wilted like a flower in the cold of the winter surrounding us. His small fists beat the gravel beneath us. I crawled from my spot in the gravel to him and embraced his trembling body. What in the world had just happened? What in the world had just become of us? We cried while screaming into each other, broken-hearted. I had no idea how to function from here.

Thoughts came to my mind that soon our family would arrive, and they could not find us crumpled in the gravel. I helped Conner to his feet. He screamed through his tears, "Well, my life sucks now because I don't have a dad!"

As we walked toward the house, each helping to hold the other up, I said, "Yes, you do, Bubba, and you always will, because Daddy will always be in your heart. We just have to rely on God right now, Conner. That's all we can do."

We stopped before we reached the door when Conner vomited. I wiped my face and entered survival mode. I had to survive this for my son. I had to help wipe his vomit and tears and get him into the house.

I explained that the police were coming to check on us. I explained that this was a routine in accidents. We prayed hard for strength. We stood in the gravel beside our front door. I held on to my little boy's shoulders and prayed aloud, "God, whatever is going on, whatever has happened," I still did not believe or accept the news, "please give us strength. Lord, we need you now more than we ever have. Please God, please." And with that we entered our home.

I paced between the kitchen table, the one where my husband had last sat, and the sliding glass door. I looked toward the road to see if the police vehicles were on their way.

Very soon they were. One white SUV and one dark blue patrol car raced toward our house as the gravel flew behind them. Conner and I went outside to meet them. The highway patrol car was driven by a local man, Evan.

I said, "No, Evan! This can't be true! It can't be!" I almost fell to the ground. He collected me and said we needed to go inside. Evan helped my son and me back into our home. He sat adjacent to me at the kitchen table as I held my head in my hands in disbelief.

I called my mom and said simply, "Mom, I need you to come home. Mike is dead and I can't talk, but please just come, Mom, please. I love you."

I texted my sister Amy because I couldn't speak anymore. My sister's response to my text was simple: **Oh my God. I'm on my way. I love you.**

Amy was in Branson, normally a three-hour drive. My brother-in-law told me later that Amy and the girls made it in about two.

After I contacted Mom and Amy, I sat again with my head resting in my hands. Conner paced the floor from the living room to the kitchen. He no longer cried. He checked on me. He came to me and kissed my head. He hugged whoever entered our home. He became a man in those moments. He became his mother's protector. Everything else was oblivious to me.

My dad arrived first, and then Chris and Gayle, Mike's mom and stepdad. Chris saw the highway patrol and deputy standing in our kitchen. She broke down and fell, screaming Michael's name, and my heart broke all over again. My heart ached for her. And it still aches for her now.

The next to arrive were my stepson and his mom. My eyes rose to meet his as he entered the kitchen. I hugged him and kept telling him how sorry I was. I broke two boys' hearts that day with the news of Mike's death.

Everyone exchanged hugs, and we all cried, still shocked. I repeated to every person I hugged, "I'm sorry, I'm so sorry." I could not stop saying it. I was so sorry this had happened. I was so sorry my husband was gone. I was so sorry and did not know how to say anything else.

Chris stepped into the utility room to call Mike's sister, Becky, who lives in Texas. We had known each other back in high school. It had been good to rekindle that friendship when years earlier her brother and I fell in love. Becky often told the story of when Mike decided to ask me on a date. He had called his sister to ask if she remembered me, and what she thought about me. Fortunately, she remembered me fondly and supported Mike's decision with happiness and excitement.

Evan wrote the coroner's name on a piece of paper and told me to call him if I had any questions. I knew I wouldn't call him but accepted the number anyway. I asked about Mike being brought to Erik's funeral home, and Evan said that was already being take care of. Erik had been contacted and he would be calling me later.

It all seemed unreal. I existed in a fog. I felt like I didn't exist at all. This was not me. I became someone different. At one point, I threw a cup across the kitchen and yelled. I was so angry, shocked and scared. Later, I felt like an idiot for behaving that way in front of two police officers and my son, but I had no control. There was no stability in my hands, in my voice, in my breathing, or in my reality.

The deputy from the county sheriff's department retrieved the pieces of broken cup and lid from the kitchen floor. I quietly whispered, "I'm sorry. Just . . . just throw it away."

That is how grief operates, whether it is fresh or has remained for years. The stages of grief wipe your slate clean of any previous stability you may have established. I believed that life was stable up until the news of Mike's death. All of it disappeared with the December frost.

Evan and the deputy, whose name I don't remember, left soon after. Evan later sent me a text to check on us. I appreciated that I hadn't received confirmation of my husband's death from a stranger.

After the officers left, I walked to my recliner in the main living room. I sunk into the chair, and this is where I stayed for the remainder of the day and into the evening.

Soon my mom arrived, and the house began to flood with visitors. Mom came to me with tears streaming down her face. She held on to her baby girl, who was more broken than she had ever seen. Mom hugged her grandson, her only grandson, and repeated, "I'm so sorry, Conner. I love you." My mom has suffered plenty of heartache of her own over her lifetime. But nothing compares to the suffering she felt watching her child fall apart and suffer.

Once the shock wore off, I would know that suffering. I still know it. Every time my little boy cries and throws up from an anxiety attack, a piece of me dies. Every time he tells me he misses his dad and that he cannot believe he has to grow up without him, a piece of me dies. I sometimes wonder if, soon, all of the pieces of me will be gone.

Every person who entered my broken home wore a look of despair. They were heartbroken and did not know what to say. They saw me sitting in a chair, with swollen red eyes, shaking hands, and a box of tissues next to me. I was a shell of myself. Each one came straight to my chair and offered hugs and love. I met their eyes, shed unstoppable tears, and thanked them through broken sobs.

When one of my friends, Erica, arrived, she fell to her knees in front of me. I screamed and sobbed into her shoulder. We cried and embraced.

Shock and numbness consumed me. I could not feel my extremities. I didn't know what food, drinks, and other items were filling my kitchen; I only knew that every visitor provided something to sustain us and our houseful of family and friends in the days to come. Hours passed, but it felt like seconds. I sat in the same chair, cried endless tears, greeted guests, and asked where my son was every five seconds, until daylight faded.

At one point, I asked someone to check the dirty clothes hamper for an item of Mike's. I needed to hold something that still smelled like him. A dirty pair of Carhartt jeans became my crutch for the night. I folded them around my arm and never let them go. They smelled of dirt and hard work, a scent I have grown to crave. The jeans were stained and tattered around the leg hems, and they smelled of cow manure. They were soft and reminded me of the many pairs of jeans I'd bought Mike over the years. I buried my face into them many times that evening. I inhaled deeply, and with every breath, a memory increased my sobs.

I will never know this smell again. I will never have his dirty jeans to wash after I had complained of the concrete set into them, or the dried manure that dropped off when he threw them into the hamper. I will never have this again. I will never have him again. It all began to sink in.

Conner seemed to be handling the news better than me at this point. When I started wailing he would come to the back or the side of the recliner and tell me softly, "It's gonna be okay, Momma . . . you're okay." The shock would later wear off, and all hell would break loose within my son's heart. But at that moment, he remained a pillar of strength.

What amazing strength the Lord placed in our son that day. I could not function, and there he was, ten years old, comforting me. He was the one who reassured me we were going to be okay; he is the one who came to the chair and calmly and sweetly reminded me of his love.

I could not move. I could not rise from that recliner without help. I could not breathe for very long without being interrupted by sporadic bursts of sobs. I was helplessly crippled by the loss of my husband, with whom I had been in love for thirteen years. I felt completely and irreparably broken.

I remember the second my sister Amy walked across the threshold of my once happy and full home. In that instant, I realized it was no longer *our* home; it was mine. I would live in it alone with my son, Conner. Amy walked in slowly and our eyes met. She handed Reagan, her two-year-old daughter, off to my brother-in-law Merlyn, and came straight to me. Amy's oldest daughter, Alyssa, stood by her stepdad Merlyn and watched her aunt fall apart. My sister fell to her knees beside my recliner, and I broke down again. She cried right back.

"Amy, I just don't understand. I don't know what I'm going to do. How did this happen?" I uttered through broken breaths.

"I don't know, Roni Lynn. I don't know and I'm so sorry."

My sister is almost three years my senior. We fought as kids but in all our sibling rivalry, we leaned upon each other in our deepest, darkest moments. In the hours and days to come, Amy was the one who would wipe my tears and cool my swollen and tired face with a cold washcloth. She is the one who would pay our bills to get us through the first few months, and she would ensure everything had its proper place. Amy is the one who would make countless trips to town to meet with various people concerning those bills. She remained beside me from the moment she entered my home that awful day; and if she left my side long enough to attend to her own daughters, she raced back to me as soon as a new breakdown began.

A heartbeat other than my own, the one of grief, overpowered my own heartbeat. I felt the slow, aching crawl from the pit of my stomach as its claws gripped every organ and fiber within my body. I grew increasingly warm, yet shivered uncontrollably; my breathing became rapid and shallow. My cheeks flushed, and I sobbed. I could not breathe well, nor speak. Someone, usually my sister, rushed to me with a cold wet cloth. These breakdowns came often in the first few weeks. I later learned they were panic attacks. I still suffer them occasionally, even years later.

Within a couple of hours from the final confirming call, my phone rang with a call from our friend Erik, the funeral director. He reported that Mike had arrived at the funeral home. It was almost five p.m. and so I asked Erik if he thought I should have someone drive me in to see my husband then or wait until morning. He said that since it was late, and I was already so drained, it would probably be best to wait.

I decided to take Erik's advice and asked him to explain to me how this happened.

He spoke in a tender voice. "He took a pretty hard hit to the head, and he doesn't look like Mike anymore."

I asked, "What would you do if you were me? Should I see my husband's face or spare myself the pain?"

After Erik said again that Mike didn't look like Mike, I decided I could not see his face. I could not have the memory of my handsome, perfect husband tarnished. My mind raced back to that first flirtatious encounter at the Jolly Cone. That smile. That walk. That face.

I saw his shining smile, his hazel eyes, the salt-and-pepper whiskers, the scar above his left eye, and the wrinkles that had formed over the years. I could not comprehend how I would handle seeing his beauty and perfection tarnished. A few nights later, I would experience a nightmare of what I imagined his face and head looked like. It still haunts me today.

In the evening hours, Mike's sister Becky and her family arrived from Texas. I was too exhausted to stand. I remained locked in my recliner unless someone helped me to the restroom. I was unable to rise to greet any more guests; they all came straight to me. Someone placed a kitchen chair beside me for guests so Becky sat there a while, taking my sister's place momentarily, and we held hands and cried together.

Phillip, who family calls P.R., is Mike's brother who had been estranged from Mike for a few years. P.R. arrived with one of my cousins.

P.R. and Mike have had more than their share of ups and downs over the years, so I knew guilt was weighing on P.R. He sat beside me and I hugged him, telling him I was glad he came. In a broken voice he said, "I should have come a long time ago."

"Yeah, you should have, but you can't think about that now," I said. "Mike is proud of you for coming, and right now just remember your brother. Forgive him, forgive yourself, and remember him, P.R." He nodded his head in agreement.

The rest of that first night is a blur. Friends and family poured into our home, many of them for the first time. Our little boy Conner stayed strong through the entire night. He held me up more than I held him. I felt guilty, but I couldn't stop the sobs or the moments of utter disbelief. I shook uncontrollably, with frequent breakdowns. The only time they slowed was after another of my best friends, Michelle, who is a nurse practitioner at a local clinic, had thought to prescribe me some Xanax. I had never before taken an anti-depressant or any medication of that sort. I was prescribed two Xanax every several hours, and since I was inexperienced with that type of medication, they had a high effect on me. I grew tired and weak. But, they did not stop the pain. Nothing could stop the pain; the medication only numbed my body. My shell. Not my broken heart and soul.

At one point our then-preacher, Brother Johnny Gipson, and his wife, Joy, arrived. They spoke words of love to me. I remember telling Johnny I was not angry with God, despite my overwhelming feelings of anger toward God earlier in the day. I had grown so tired over the hours, and my thoughts toward God turned to begging Him for peace for my son and me. I wanted to make sure Johnny knew I was not angry; I wanted to make sure everyone knew that.

My sister said something to me days later that I did not accept in the beginning, but that brought me some comfort later. She suggested that maybe God had taken Mike because life on Earth was getting too hard for him and he deserved rest. My husband worked harder than any person I have ever known. As difficult as it has been to lose the love of my life, I know God had a reason for taking him. I may not understand it, or like it, for my own selfish reasons, but I think God took Mike because he was so tired.

He was exhausted beyond the normal realm of exhaustion; he owed money (most of which I was unaware of until forced to deal with it after his passing); he could never stop working if he wanted to pay his debts; he rarely had time to enjoy his family. Mike's workaholic lifestyle had left him drained, physically, emotionally, and spiritually. God was ready to give Mike the rest he deserved but had never received on Earth.

I am a Christian. I believe in the Lord, in Heaven, and in asking forgiveness for our sins. I believe that Jesus Christ died for me, and I believe that my husband, once his spirit left his body, had a moment with God for one last chance at redemption.

I believe when Mike met our Creator, and He asked Mike if he was sorry for all he had done in this world, that Mike fell to his knees, cried tears of love and sorrow and answered, "Yes." I envision the Lord wrapping His arms around my husband and welcoming him into His eternal home. Maybe I'm wrong, and maybe none of that took place. But maybe, just maybe, I'm right.

I picture my husband wiping the tears from his eyes as he walked alongside the Lord, and then once they entered the gates, Mike smiled. I see sunshine and warmth enveloping them both. I see Mike's eyes light up with glee as he saw his dad, Bob, in the distance. Happiness. Pure bliss. Rest. That is the image I hold on to.

When the crowds left, it was only my mom, my sister, and her family, with Conner and me. We planned to visit the funeral home first thing the next morning.

The time arrived to choose Mike's burial clothes. Earlier in the day I had considered his Marine dress uniform, and my nephew Austin had climbed into the attic to find it. But I realized I wanted to save Mike's Marine uniform for his boys. I would dress my husband in what he wore almost every single day: Carhartt jeans, a flannel shirt, his faded brown leather belt, and lace-up work boots.

I chose his newer pair of work boots because I could not stand the thought of putting on the ones he had been wearing when he was taken from us. My mom, the amazing woman that she is, ironed his clothes for me. She wanted to make sure her son-in-law looked his best.

As night descended and the Xanax settled into my system, I needed help walking to our bedroom. Our son took his dad's place in our king-sized bed and would sleep there for as long as he wanted. Conner fell asleep quickly, but my mind would not shut down. I prayed. I cried. I tossed and turned.

My muscles ached. My heart ached. My soul ached.

As I lay there silently sobbing, I heard my bedroom door softly open. My sister scooted into bed beside me and held me, crying into my shoulder. We talked for a while. I cried and recounted how I could not believe this was happening. I whispered my biggest fears to her. What would happen to us? How in the world did we get here? I *just* had him. He was just here, alive and well. She laid with me for a long while, her arm wrapped around me tightly. In time, she left to return to Conner's room to check on Reagan. Alyssa, my other niece, who would be fourteen in six days, and my mom slept in another bed. I know the night was restless for everyone.

Chapter Seven

Unable to sleep, I rose early the next morning, Mike's dirty Carhartt jeans still tangled in my arms. I entered Mike's office. I saw his farm coat draped over the office chair. Matt, one of our farm hands, had retrieved the coat from Mike's truck that had been left parked at the concrete plant where he died. I fell into my husband's office chair, a new one I had bought for him recently, and wrapped Mike's coat around my arm. I sank into his chair and sobbed so hard that I woke my brother-in-law, Merlyn. He came into the office, knelt in front of me, and let me cry into him.

Conner woke soon after. I sat in the recliner, unable to move for a long time. I sat and stared. I cried for a while and then formed my blank stare again. I was numb and still reeling from the shock. It was December 30, and in only minutes, I would enter the funeral home to see my husband.

I sent Erik a text that read: **Can you make it so I can hold my husband's hand without having to see his face? I just need to hold his hand.**

He replied: **Yes, I can make that work.**

Because Mike did not look like himself due to the damage to his head, I still chose not to see his face, but I wanted to hold his hand so badly. I missed his hands. Mike's hands were large and usually swollen with bruises or cuts. Callouses covered the palms below his fingers and arthritis had begun to bother him. His joints ached and his fingers would swell. His hands were perfect and beautiful.

They held our boys with love. They helped form a life worth living. Mike's hands held mine and provided comfort and safety when needed. They held discipline and command when required. I miss his hands on the small of my back. I miss his hands holding mine. I miss his hands playing with Matchbox cars in the floor with his boys.

The morning seemed to creep by, but the time finally came to leave for the funeral home. I wanted family to be as much a part of the decision making for arrangements as they wanted, so I asked my stepson and Mike's family to meet me at the funeral home. Mom drove Conner and me. I was still weak and needed help walking, but I hugged my stepson as soon as he crossed the parking lot. I told him again how sorry I was and that I loved him. I told him if he wanted his mom there, she was welcome. I told him to text her. He did, and said she arrived a little while later.

We all entered the double doors and climbed the stairs. Remembering the experience, my stomach becomes nauseated and my heart beats quickly.

Erik met us and hugged me, and told me again how sorry he was. He and Mike had been really close right around the time Mike and I began dating. Erik and his wife, Farrah, and Mike and I used to go out together.

I'll never forget the time Erik, Mike and I left a local bar after Mike's step-grandfather's visitation. We had all needed some relaxation after the day, and Mike called Erik to meet us. We enjoyed the evening with dancing and a few beers. As the night wore on, Mike expressed his desire to go skinny dipping. Yes, in the middle of town, he wanted to go skinny dipping.

So, Erik, Mike and I drove my truck to the river access, and my insanely non-bashful husband (boyfriend at the time) undressed right in front of Erik and me. I was so embarrassed, but Erik and Mike just laughed! Michael kicked off his boots then removed his white button-down shirt and khakis. He ran toward the river without a stitch of clothing on and dove into the cold Current River.

Erik laughed, and I stood there with my mouth agape and my beer in my hand, hoping and praying no one would drive by and see us.

The skinny dipping only lasted a little while, and sure enough, as soon as Mike exited the water, I saw headlights in the distance. A city police car pulled down to the river access just in time for Michael to get his pants on, and get his shirt on but draped open. I was afraid we'd be ticketed, but instead, the officer just asked Mike if we were all doing okay.

Mike laughed, grinned that amazing and mischievous grin and said, "You bet."

As I ventured, shaky and weak, up the stairs of the funeral home, Erik asked if I was ready to see Mike. As soon as he said it I crumpled to the floor, crying and screaming that I couldn't believe he was gone. Nothing about life seemed real. My breathing quickened and became shallow again, my palms were sweaty and shaking, my entire body felt unable to function.

I finally composed myself as best I could and was helped into a standing position. I still had Mike's farm coat wrapped around my left arm.

"As soon as I open the door, you're going to see him, okay?" Erik looked so pained to have to do this for his friend's wife.

"Okay." I barely breathed, not wanting to take one step forward.

"Are you ready?"

I nodded my head. I'm unsure who was on either side of me, holding me up. I breathed deeply and we stepped into the room.

On a cold metal table, covered in a white sheet, except for his left forearm and hand, was my husband. I collapsed again, screaming and sobbing. My dad and Erik helped me drag myself to the table.

How in the world is this really happening? I reached for his hand; it felt so cold. I noticed two horizontal indentations on his arm. I rubbed my right hand over them, fearing they were marks from the concrete truck hitting him. Anger instantly entered my heart.

Why in the hell did he buy that godforsaken concrete plant? I wanted to shout it to the rooftops. Screams formed within me and longed to escape from my soul; but instead I sobbed and cried loudly, "*Why?*"

A few days later, Erik explained those marks were from the embalming table and completely unrelated to Mike's injuries.

I hated to think of the pain Mike must have felt. I imagined only the worst images of how he had died. I imagined the concrete chute and the mixer spinning and spinning, while his body was trapped. I imagined him being completely alone at the concrete plant, and I was angry that I hadn't been there. I was angry that no one else had been there. He should not have been alone. Had someone been there to help him, maybe my husband, a loving father of two, would not be lying cold on that table. Maybe I would not be a widow.

My mind imagined his final thought. Was it guilt? Fear? Anger? I pray his final thought was of the love we shared as a family: him, me, and our boys. But I fear his final thought was anger that he slipped and fell, or anger that his clothing became entangled and pulled him in. I worry that his final thought was anger that he had allowed himself to become tangled. *How could I be so careless,* I imagined him thinking. *How could I have been too busy to spend more time with my family?* I worried that his final thought was fear about what would happen to his wife and children. How were we going to handle this loss? Or perhaps he simply thought, *I'm sorry.*

No one will ever know my husband's final thoughts, or if he made a sound when death quickly grasped him. He was all by himself at the plant; no one was there to see him slip and to pull him back. No one was there to keep him from being hit by the machine, over and over again. I blame myself. I blame others. I blame Mike and his desire for more, more, more. But more than blame, sorrow overpowers my heart.

I often wish that Conner and I had surprised Mike with lunch that day, and then maybe it would never have happened. But deep down, I think it would have happened no matter what. Had Conner and I been there to surprise Mike, we would have witnessed the tragedy and found it impossible to heal.

After I saw my lifeless husband for the first time, my thoughts returned to the task at hand: holding his hand and then choosing his casket. I cried onto Mike's hand and I whispered to him, "I'm so sorry babe, I'm so sorry this happened to you . . . I love you . . . I love you . . . I love you. I'm so sorry . . . I'm so sorry, babe . . . I can't believe this happened to you . . . I'm so sorry . . ."

I repeated these words many times, and as I held my head to his hand, my knees buckled beneath me. I think my dad and Erik held me up the whole time, one on either arm. I rested my head on Mike's chest. *Why won't his heart beat again? Why won't his chest rise and fall with his breaths? How did this happen? How did we get here?*

I kissed my gentle husband's hand and told him I loved him once more before I turned to allow Chris and Becky to say their goodbyes. I heard Becky tell Chris, "No, not yet . . ." Becky later told me Chris was crying Mike's name and she wanted to see his face. Becky was afraid Chris would turn back the sheet too soon and that I would see Mike's face as well.

After I was safely out of sight, Chris pulled back the sheet and kissed Mike's face. Later, I asked her how he looked. She said his face was swollen because of the blood that had rushed to his head as he lay on the edge of the concrete truck after impact. She said it looked like the blows came to the right side of his face and head. I closed my eyes tightly, trying to diminish the image that flashed in front of me. I could not fathom my poor husband's death. I hated it. I still hate it, but part of me regrets not seeing his face. I wonder now if seeing his face would have helped bring me closure.

The morning continued in a melancholy charade of answering questions and choosing funeral arrangements. Numbness overwhelmed me with all the questions and decisions. We spent some time in the discussion room answering questions about dates, places, and names for the obituary, and then the time came to choose a casket.

A mother should never have to bury her child. A son should not have to make arrangements to bury his father the day after his eighteenth birthday. A thirty-six-year old woman should not have to choose a casket or make these kinds of decisions regarding the love of her life. But we three—my mother-in-law, Mike's firstborn son, and I—were here doing these terrible things. At the same time, we were there for each other. That did not make any of it easier, but it helped to know none of us were alone in the process. I am grateful that my stepson and his mom helped; I cannot imagine how difficult it must have been for them.

As we crossed the hallway to re-enter the room where my husband had been a few minutes before, my knees again grew weak. As soon as I looked at the caskets, I knew which one looked "like Mike" on the outside. Crafted from old barn wood, the rustic casket offered a sad and beautiful welcome. I pointed to that one, and as Erik slid it out for us to view and then lifted the lid, my eyes fell upon an embroidered farm scene. I fell to the ground again, grasping the casket and sobbing. I was in complete disbelief that we were here choosing a casket for my husband. My hands ran over the weathered wood and felt the stark contrast of the cream silk interior.

I asked my stepson if he thought the barn wood casket was okay. He said in the sweetest voice, the same way he answered all questions that day, "Yes, ma'am." How I love that child like my own. My heart broke further whenever I looked at either of our boys those first few days and weeks. *How was I going to raise our son Conner on my own? How was my stepson going to begin college without his dad's advice? How were they going to survive this tragedy?* My thoughts ran wild with these fears every time I looked into their eyes. Their innocence and happiness were shattered the day they lost their dad; the day we lowered him in the ground just confirmed that life would never be the same.

One more time, I ran my fingers across the embroidered farm scene inside the lid of the casket, and then we went to view the guest books and obituary programs. We chose a matching farm set. A beautiful open field with a round hay bale adorned the front of the guest book and obituary programs. It was perfect for my husband.

    We finally reached these important decisions and returned to the discussion room. Hours passed as we continued to answer questions and make decisions. A rough draft of the obituary was typed and a few of us made minor corrections. When the morning finally ended, I was completely and utterly drained and exhaustion began to take its toll. We all said our goodbyes and each headed to our own homes. This was Tuesday, December 30. Since my stepson's eighteenth birthday was on Wednesday, December 31, the visitation and funeral would take place on Thursday, January 1, 2015, beginning at eleven a.m.

Chapter Eight

The next day Conner and his brother planned to go to their Nanny Chris's house to visit with their cousins, Billy and Derek, Becky's boys. When my stepson arrived, I gave him an old photo album I found in Mike's office. The album contained pictures of his parents when they were dating.

I also found his dad's high school class ring and Marine Corps ring and gave him first choice of rings since it was his birthday. He chose the class ring from high school. I told Conner that his daddy's Marine Corps ring would be his one day, but I would like to wear it for a while if that was okay. He agreed and then the boys left the house. Conner told me later that his brother took him to Pleasant Site Cemetery before going to their Nanny's. He wanted to show Conner where their dad would be buried the following day.

After taking a nap, I asked Matt, our farm hand, to drive me to Chris and Gayle's so I could be with the boys. I visited in the kitchen with Becky, Bill, Chris, Grandma Mary, and Gayle. I still do not know how Chris managed to hold herself together as well as she did. She faked it, I'm sure. I have gotten pretty good at faking "normal" and "okay" as well.

Grandma Mary is Chris's mom and Mike's maternal grandma. She is always the life of the family gatherings with her laughter and sense of humor. Everyone was quiet, but still in pleasant moods with their conversation, none of which was too sad. I think they were all trying to keep my spirits as high as possible, not wanting to flood my mind with more sadness and fear. They laughed and shared stories, and then our renter arrived.

We owned a rental property up the road from Chris and Gayle's; it is the house to which we brought Conner home. Mike bought the property one year before we married, fixed it up, and we moved into the house when I was seven months pregnant with Conner. It is a tiny house, with nothing modern, but it was cozy and fine for the few years we lived there. We moved back to our old Garwood farm when Conner was three.

The old Garwood farm is the one I wish we had kept. It was one hundred eighty-two acres and plenty big enough; I was hesitant when Mike decided to buy the big farm in Fremont, where we currently live. I was nervous about purchasing the big farm of twelve hundred acres, but no matter how much I pleaded with that man, once he set his mind to something, it would happen one way or another.

Our renter came in and sat at the kitchen table with us. She had the rent money to give me, but said things were not going well with her family, so she might be late on the rent some months. She had been late with the rent every month, and I used to complain to Mike about it. However, her story gave me a little insight. She told me her husband had just been diagnosed with stage three colon cancer, and she was a cancer survivor herself.

"I'm so sorry to hear that. I hope you guys find answers and he heals from this," I said.

She looked at me and said, "I appreciate it, but at least I still have my husband. You're the one who needs the sympathy. Tomorrow, you are burying your husband. I still have mine, even though he has cancer."

Regardless of her good intentions, I could not leave the room fast enough. I went to the back room where the boys were playing Nintendo. I took a small pillow and Mike's coat, which remained tightly coiled around my arm, and lay on the floor to watch the four of them, some almost grown men, play an old Nintendo like they were all little boys. I snuggled with Mike's coat and lay silently watching them enjoy being together.

Over the years we spent many summers with Becky, Bill, and their boys. We played on Current River, camped, floated, and attended family reunions. The boys had grown close over the years of spending summers and Christmases together. Due to work schedules, Becky and her family had not been able to visit Missouri very often, so the boys had not seen each other in a long while. Laughter filled the room as they all teased each other and played Nintendo.

I lay there watching them while we chatted casually, all such good boys. They had worked alongside Mike. The older boys had worked in the hay fields for years, picked up rocks when they were too young to drive a truck or a tractor, and earned money through their work for Mike.

Becky joined us in the back room and lay beside me on the floor. We listened to our boys have fun and forget the terrible sadness for a while. Soon evening approached, and my exhaustion settled in again. Also, that tangible feeling of emptiness and sadness that rears its ugly head still to this day began to take hold. I knew it was time to go when I developed the familiar feeling in my stomach. My breath labored and the uncontrollable shaking gripped me once more. Becky and her husband Bill drove me home.

I was so nervous about the following morning. I wanted everything to be perfect, but I dreaded every second. How in the world was I going to lay my husband in the ground?

My preacher, Brother Johnny Gipson, visited to ask if I had any special requests for the service. I told him I wanted it to be over quickly. I could not deal with dragging the sadness out. It needed to be quick and to the point. He asked if I had any special verses. I requested Ecclesiastes. I have always found the flow of the verse beautiful:

There is a time for everything, and a season for every activity under the heavens:

a time to be born and a time to die, a time to plant and a time to uproot,

a time to kill and a time to heal, a time to tear down and a time to build,

a time to weep and a time to laugh, a time to mourn and a time to dance,

a time to scatter stones and a time to gather them, a time to embrace and a time to refrain from embracing,

a time to search and a time to give up, a time to keep and a time to throw away,

a time to tear and a time to mend, a time to be silent and a time to speak,

a time to love and a time to hate, a time for war and a time for peace.

Isn't it beautiful how all things bad turn into all things pure and perfect? That's what I know happened when Mike arrived in Heaven. He had his conversation with God and then all things sad, exhausting, lonely, worrisome, and terrible turned to pure happiness.

Chapter Nine

MORNING ARRIVED AND BROUGHT WITH IT THE MOST difficult day of our lives. Conner later said that Monday, December 29, the day Mike died, was the worst day of his life and Thursday, January 1, the day of Mike's funeral, the hardest. I agree.

Conner dressed in what we call his "church jeans," the dark wash, stain-free kind, and a button up, plaid, collared shirt. We combed his hair as best we could. I asked my brother-in-law, Merlyn, to be an honorary pallbearer and chose one of Mike's plaid shirts for him to wear.

The two of them had shared many laughs over the years. Merlyn loved Mike like a brother, and Mike the same for him. I asked all the pallbearers to wear jeans, a flannel or plaid shirt, and a belt; that was Mike's typical ensemble. I told Merlyn he looked handsome in Mike's shirt and he could keep it. He said he felt very honored, and tough, to wear Mike's shirt.

I chose a black sweater and a new pair of gray dress pants that my mom had given me as a Christmas present. I wore flat black dress shoes that I purchased the week before. My hair was unkempt, so I brushed it free of tangles and pulled it into a low ponytail. The only jewelry I wore was Mike's Marine Corps ring around my neck and my wedding ring. No makeup covered my face.

My dad requested to drive us.

Both the visitation and funeral took place at South Van Buren General Baptist Church. A brunch was served at ten a.m. At eleven a.m., the family would go upstairs for our time with Mike, then visitation would be open to the public starting at noon. The funeral would follow at two p.m.

When we arrived at the church, I grew sick to my stomach with nerves. No part of me wanted to enter the sacred building or participate in saying goodbye. I was numb, avoiding eye contact with as many people as possible, only looking at my son and close family members. I could not stand the sad and pitiful looks given to me. This was my reality now and it was awful, terrible, and scary. The looks of pity still affect me to this day. I often wonder if people fear I will have an emotional breakdown at any moment.

I sat at a table facing away from the door to further avoid eye contact. Conner sat to my right, my parents, my sister, and close family surrounding us. Someone asked if I wanted food, but I declined, as usual. Once a few more people arrived, I told someone to go ahead and ask a church member or Brother Johnny to bless the food so people could eat. I drank a small glass of orange juice.

I sat nervously awaiting the time to go upstairs. Both our boys looked so handsome as they sat on either side of me. I could not believe how grown up they seemed. I still hate that their dad doesn't get to be here with them anymore.

Finally, Erik came downstairs and told me that if I was ready, I could go up to be with Mike. I asked him if he could please prepare him one more time so I could hold his hand like at the funeral home. He agreed and quickly disappeared back upstairs.

I asked the boys if they wanted to join me, but they both declined. I took a deep breath to prepare myself. Watchful eyes followed my every move as my sister and mom rose with me. I needed help walking up the steps, so my sister held on to me and guided me up. As I ascended the top step, my breathing became erratic again and I broke down. Every step felt like a mountain I was ill-prepared to climb.

There were pictures of him everywhere . . . beautiful, heartbreaking pictures. There were pictures of Mike and our boys, all smiling with unsuspecting happiness. Pictures of Mike and me on our wedding day and during our first few months together adorned the foyer table. A small board containing photos from Mike's childhood stood on an easel. I could not look at the pictures directly, but only darted my eyes quickly across them for fear of passing out if I gazed too long.

Erik stood at the double entry doors. The glass had been covered with white paper to offer the family privacy before allowing the public inside. "Now, when I open these you'll be able to see him, okay? He's ready, but you need to know you'll see him as soon as you walk in. Are you ready?"

I nodded and in a weak and weary whisper replied, "Yes." I averted my eyes to the floor.

The doors opened; I slowly lifted my gaze. Beautiful flowers surrounded his casket. Our picture of Mike and the boys from when Conner was only two adorned the top. I sobbed all the way to the casket. I held one of our wedding pictures in my hand, his farm coat still wrapped tightly around my arm. Each step took pains to complete. It felt as if my feet dragged themselves into position against my will. I did not want to move forward. I did not want to touch that casket again. I did not want my husband's hand to be cold and lifeless. My feet forged ahead regardless.

When I arrived, I reached for Mike's hand. Both hands were folded one on top of the other, and nestled behind them were the two pictures I had chosen of our boys. I wanted him to have a picture of each of his sons with him. I shakily slid our wedding photo under the boys' pictures. I held Mike's hand and rested my head upon his chest. I longed to hear his heartbeat, but nothing but the sound of my own sobs rang through my ears. I wanted to feel his chest rise and fall. I confessed my love and cried again about how sorry I was this had happened. I said those things over and over and sobbed with every breath. I held his hand tightly and then kissed it.

"I love you so much and I promise I'll do my best," I said. I was helped to the front pew. Erik made eye contact with me, I nodded affirmation, and a moment later, Mike's casket was closed. This was the last time I saw my husband.

I wanted him out of that casket, alive and well, for one last time. I wanted to lie down beside him with his arm wrapped around me like it used to be. I wanted to hear and feel him breathing. I wanted our fingers to intertwine, and I wanted to kiss his soft lips. I wanted to hear him say, "I love you, babe," one more time. I wanted to tell him, "I'm sorry," and for him to hear it. I wanted it to be a few days before and for him to not have gone to work that day. I wanted to protect our boys from this tragedy. I wanted to rewind and take it all back. I wanted to hear him flirt with me once more, to feel his hands around my waist.

I could not have any of those things I longed for, but it did not lessen that longing. I wanted the love of my life back. For him to be alive and right next to me. I wanted to hear his laugh and see the sparkle in his eyes. A part of me died in that church where I had spent many Sundays. When that lid closed I felt like I could no longer breathe, just as Mike couldn't. The finality of the closed lid overwhelmed me, confirmed again at the grave later that afternoon.

I'm unsure how much time passed before I sent someone to see if the boys were ready to join me. When they joined me on the front pew, I broke down again. I told them both how much I loved them and kept asking if they were doing okay. They silently nodded, and Conner sometimes cried. As more time passed in a blur, I told someone to get the rest of the family to join us. I asked Erik if he would arrange chairs by the casket, because I knew I was not strong enough to greet everyone while standing. He placed three chairs at the front for me and the boys. Neither wanted to sit there, so my sister, my mom, Chris, and Becky took turns sitting beside me.

It seemed like only a matter of minutes passed when Erik approached me. "I know it's a little early, but is it okay to go ahead and let people in?" he asked. "There are a lot of people waiting to pay their respects, many who are good friends. A line has already formed and several people are standing outside in the cold."

I took a deep breath and whispered, "Yes." I made sure the boys were okay again and that they both had someone right next to them. I was helped to the first chair, where I sat with Mike's coat still tightly wound around my arm. As my eyes reached the back doors, Erik opened them. It was like a floodgate had been opened.

There was already a crowd gathered in the foyer, and as the doors opened wide, they all looked nervous. They had not been prepared to lose Mike either. One by one, for more than two hours, friends, family, coworkers, current students, former students, and even strangers paid their respects. At one point, I raised my head to see the high school boys' basketball team, all in a line, each dressed the same, with the coach and assistant coach leading the line. That moved my heart tremendously. They did that as a team for my stepson.

The line never stopped or slowed. People poured in constantly, with the line extending outside. The side rooms of the church were opened for people to stand or sit. The walls were lined with people who could not find a seat after they made their way through the line. I noticed some standing in the back, who had not made it through the line at all.

At the end of the two hours, I was exhausted. I had not used the restroom since arriving, so I asked Becky to help me go there. I kept my eyes down to avoid eye contact; I did the same on my way back up the aisle.

I sat for a little while longer in the chair at the front before asking Erik if he could ask Brother Johnny to start the funeral a few minutes early. It was almost two o'clock, and I felt exhausted and drained beyond anything I've ever known.

Brother Johnny obliged; the chairs were removed, and I was helped to the front pew seat. This time I sat between our boys, with my parents and sister behind us. The three of them were crying during the funeral, and their hands never left my shoulders. I felt their love and their sadness. It killed them to see me suffering. They felt helpless in comforting me, just as I felt helpless in comforting our boys. How do you heal a heart so broken and shattered by such a tragic loss?

You pray. You listen. You hold on tight, and you let go when necessary.

Brother Johnny began the service, spoke a few words, and then, "Go Rest High on That Mountain" by Vince Gill and Patty Loveless played. I cried. I heard sniffling and crying throughout the church. I held on to our boys. My chest tightened and my hands shook the entire time. Both boys cried sporadically, and I heard sniffles from my parents and sister right behind me. I pictured my husband with every word of that song. I pictured him standing atop the mountain, sunshine caressing his face, his smile radiating happiness. No more pain. No more sorrow. No more work.

Johnny talked of Mike kindly, although he never had the pleasure to really know him. He had greeted Mike a few times, but they did not have a relationship beyond that. Johnny said he had heard some great stories of Mike in the last few days, some of which he could not share inside a church. I heard laughter, which warmed my heart and made me smile through the tears. One such story had something to do with driving a car through a dip and all of the car's contents flying around like shrapnel. Several expletives were used in the original rendition of that story, although Brother Johnny did not repeat them.

A few more words and then "Praise You in This Storm" by Casting Crowns played. More tears flowed. My husband, our boys' father, our family's strength, was in that casket. The church overflowed with people who loved Mike and our family.

My heart flashed back to our wedding day, to the way he looked at me in my wedding dress and told me that he loved me. I then wandered back to the day we learned we were pregnant and the way my husband's hand rested on my stomach, so thankful for our miracle growing inside me. I flashed back to the day we welcomed our baby boy into this world, and how Mike's strength right beside me had gotten me through the delivery.

My husband was in that casket, and that life as I knew it was over.

I shook myself from those thoughts and my soul smiled through the pain. I praised God in my own storm. I praised Him for the years I had with my husband, and for the love of all the people who filled the church and spilled onto the outdoor patio. The front two pews were so full of love that day. Families which had been torn apart by divorce came back together to forget past differences and support each other through this tragedy. My parents had been divorced since I was two years of age, but it didn't matter on this day. Mike had been divorced for several years, but that didn't matter on this day either. We were two mothers there for our boys, all mourning the man we had loved.

Brother Johnny read from the book of Ecclesiastes and then told the crowd that I requested it be short and simple. We were led in prayer and then the last song played.

The final song surprised a few people. I had chosen a new song that our family grew to call Mike's song, which fit him perfectly: "Drinking Class" by Lee Brice. The lyrics remind me of Mike and his work ethic. Still to this day, family and friends will text me when the song plays on their radio. It begins with, "Get up when the rooster crows . . ." and it goes on to describe a man's work ethic, and how a special class of people work harder than others but enjoy their downtime. Mike loved the song, and every time it came on, he turned it up loud and listened with pride. He would say, "Turn it up, babe." He related to the lyrics, the difference being that Mike never stopped. Mike's mind always turned with work and project ideas, regardless if he was on downtime or not.

When the song finished, Erik announced, "Ladies and gentlemen, we will now carry Mike out to the foyer and his family will immediately follow. After that, you are welcome to follow, but please let us get him out first."

This was it.

My final walk with my husband.

How in the world did this happen?

Brother Johnny and Erik removed the flowers closest to the casket and turned the casket trolley so the wheels would move smoothly down the aisle. We followed close behind. When we made it to the foyer, before the pallbearers carried my husband to the hearse, I hugged each of them and said, "Thank you for carrying my husband." They humbly replied with gratitude themselves.

My truck was parked right behind the hearse. I helped Conner into the back seat, then my dad helped me into the front passenger seat. We waited a long time for everyone to get to their vehicles and for the casket flowers to make their way into the back of the hearse to ride with Mike to the graveyard. During this time, people who had not made it inside due to lack of room, paid their respects to me.

A couple of my students came to my window and told me I looked beautiful as always. I was so moved by all the love and support given to our family that day. It was amazing to see the number of people who flocked to the church. Many of them followed us to the cemetery as well. After the two boys walked away from my door, Conner cried. I asked if he wanted to ride up front between my dad and me. He nodded his head in agreement, so I opened the doors and helped him into the cab of the truck. I held on tightly and pulled him close to me.

I held my little boy, the one who came into this world as a tiny six-pound baby. I held him and his tears flowed freely and fiercely for the first time since Mike died. Conner sobbed into the sleeve of his dad's coat, which was draped over my left arm. I held on as tightly as I could and repeated over and over again, "I love you."

The hearse pulled away slowly and we followed suit. I was nauseated and felt a wave of that nervous, dreadfully sick feeling wash over me. This feeling remained for the duration of the drive. It worsened when the truck arrived at the cemetery gate.

My dad, Conner and I rode in near silence to the cemetery, but the radio was on low volume. We kept looking in the mirrors to see the line of traffic behind us; someone told us later they guessed it stretched for three miles. Since the funeral procession traveled slowly, it seemed we would never reach Pleasant Site Cemetery. As the moments ticked by, I held on to Conner as tightly as I could and wiped his tears away.

All of a sudden, I heard a familiar tune: "Drinking Class." I increased the radio's volume as Conner and I held each other and cried through the lyrics. God sent us that song. God and Mike. I have no doubt. It came on at exactly the right moment, because it ended when Dad shifted the truck to park.

Chapter Ten

I INHALED DEEPLY BEFORE GETTING OUT OF THE TRUCK. OUR dreaded walk began up the hill toward the blue tent. The wind blew wildly with temperatures in the low thirties. The weather suited how I felt: devoid of anything pleasant and hopeful, cold and stark, painful and empty. I had been holding Mike's coat and put it on against the cold. Slowly, people pulled into the cemetery lot and made the climb.

I sat between the boys again with my parents and sister behind me. We arranged for Mike to receive full Marine honors. Erik told me the Marines had gotten lost, but were now on their way. Living in the country and holding a funeral at a cemetery in the middle of a farm, obviously was not working out well for the Marines from who knows where.

We progressed slowly and hoped they would arrive in time for the flag folding. If not, then Erik and Johnny Gipson, both former Army men, would fold for us. Erik said that Mike might not like having two Army guys folding his flag, but he and Johnny would get a kick out of it. I think Mike would have grinned and shook his head with a twinkle in his eye.

It took a few minutes for everyone to make it around the tent. Erik asked people to stay behind us so when it was time for the Honor Guard to fire the rifles, the boys and I would be able to view them fully.

Once the crowd gathered, Erik gave Brother Johnny the nod to begin. I don't remember much of what Johnny said. I knew he continued to speak kind words about my husband, but I felt deaf. My senses were numbed as I held on to the boys' hands and cried. I shook uncontrollably, but not from the cold. Before I knew it, the Honor Guard readied their rifles, and fortunately, the two Marines arrived in the nick of time. They stood beside the Honor Guard and presented arms.

The gunshots rang out through the cold winter wind and my shoulders jerked with each shot. It felt like each bullet pierced my heart. Cows from the neighboring farm came toward the fence, like they, too, wanted to pay their respects to my husband.

When the gunshots settled, the two Marines walked forward to fold the flag that covered Mike's casket. They struggled with folding it. It took a few tries. I could tell they were both nervous. Their hands were covered with pristine white gloves. Their uniforms were perfectly pressed and their shoes polished to match.

Afterward, people said they could not believe how many times the Marines messed up, but I told them I held no grudges. I wanted them to realize that those Marines were having a difficult time for many reasons. They had received a call to drive hours to a funeral of a brother, they had no idea where they were going, and they had gotten lost along the way. It was freezing cold, and they had to fold this flag in front of a man's family who was falling apart.

As one of the Marines handed me the folded flag, he bent to me with one hand on top of the flag and one hand on bottom. My hands rested exactly opposite of his. He spoke kindly and quietly, expressing his apologies for my loss and thanking me for my husband's service.

I said with broken words, "Thank you so much for coming to honor my husband."

The Marine, a young man who was a stranger to me, stepped back, and he and his fellow Marine presented arms to me. I cried tears I thought would never cease as I clutched the folded flag tightly to my chest. My husband was gone. Reality dropkicked me in the throat once more, and I could not manage to swallow the lump that threatened my breaths.

Brother Johnny finished the service, and it was time for people to once again hug me and the rest of the family. People filed one by one past the boys and me.

When most everyone had gone, I noticed that my stepson had walked down the hill with his cousin, unable to be there any longer. I understood, but part of me wished he would have stayed; I wanted to hold on to him like I held onto Conner. I'm not his mom, but I love him as much as I love Conner, and I wanted to comfort him if I could. But he needed to escape, so I did not call his name.

I told Conner I wanted to stay until they had put Daddy all the way into the ground and asked if he wanted to stay. He did not, so I hugged him and kissed him goodbye. My mom drove Conner to our house. Once I was sure Conner was out of sight, it was time for me to say goodbye one final time. There were still several people standing around and I felt like a circus freak. I hated that they were watching but then again, I was happy they were seeing a true example of real love.

I looked at Erik. "Is it okay for me to say goodbye now?" I asked meekly.

He nodded his head. My sister helped me to the coffin and I hugged it, crying and shaking.

I spoke the important words to him, the ones I had spoken at the funeral home and earlier that morning in the church.

"I love you so much. I'm sorry this happened to you, babe. I wish it hadn't happened. I'm so sorry. I miss you so much already. I'm trying my best. I promise I'll do the very best I can to make you proud and to raise our boys well. I love you forever. Now, forever, and always times infinity."

This was a phrase we began using in our emails to one another during the early stages of dating. The movie *Toy Story* was popular when we dated and Buzz Lightyear was one of my stepson's favorite characters. Mike and I told each other we loved each other now, forever, and always. We added "times infinity" to our phrase after watching *Toy Story* for what seemed to be the millionth time one night. It stuck. We signed anniversary and birthday cards with NFAxI, the shortened version of the phrase.

My head rested upon the barn wood. The words flowed through broken sobs. Weakness overtook me. I did not want to let go. I did not want to leave him. No part of me accepted his death, solo parenting, financial strains, loneliness, and all that my future now held.

I gently kissed the casket and was helped back to my seat. I sobbed into the neatly folded flag. I could not breathe. I wanted to scream his name, curse to the heavens, and pound my fists into the soil beneath my feet.

Once my eyes were open and my breathing not so labored, I looked at Erik. He asked, "Are you ready?" No. My heartbeat slowed to an almost absent beat, yet it raced in the same instant. I had built a life, a home, a family with this man. And he was now about to be lowered into nothingness, into darkness that I wished would swallow me whole as well. Conner did not cross my mind in that moment; only my own loss raced through my brain. I was losing so much. I was losing everything.

I nodded as they removed the straps and lowered my husband into the ground. A cry left my throat, a cry like that of a child being ripped from his mother, only intensified beyond recognition. I reached out to the casket, as if my supernatural powers would bring him back, would lift this final resting place back to me. The pain was unreal. It was final. He was gone. They were lowering him into the ground and I would never see my husband again. I was broken. I must have cried, "No!" at one point because Erik asked, "Do you want us to keep going?"

I replied with a solemn nod. I lowered my eyes and sat there until my husband was completely lowered and there was nothing to do but fill the hole with dirt. The tears dried on my cheeks as I sat staring into the gaping hole. The cold wind ripped across those of us who remained at the cemetery. I shook partly from the freezing temperature, and partly from the shock of reality.

Acceptance.
Denial.
Fear.
Loss.
Confusion.
Anger.
Desperation.

All wrapped into one heartbeat that kept pounding with every rush of blood.

"Well, I guess that's it, huh? He's really gone," I said to my sister.

"Are you ready to go home?" Amy asked, while her arms cradled me. I nodded in agreement and we walked slowly back to my truck. She helped me into my seat and closed the door. Dad and I drove in silence.

Chapter Eleven

At our home, friends arrived later to tell stories of my husband. We filled our living room with chairs and people who loved Mike. So many stories were shared and I laughed out loud at them all. I cried in between. At times, I couldn't breathe. My sister came over and sat on my lap and held me as I wailed. Everyone went silent in those moments, and I apologized each time. Of course, my amazing friends all said I did not need to apologize and that they loved me. My breakdowns continued throughout the evening, although I relished in the happy and amazing memories everyone shared.

Stories of Mike's crazy shenanigans echoed through our living room. Laughter intermingled with tears. The stories filled our home and our hearts.

Every time I broke down, my little boy came up behind my recliner and said it would be okay. A few times it was so bad, my sister and my friends wiped my face with a cold, wet washcloth. I hyperventilated and felt I might pass out. I'm grateful those incidents did not make up the whole night, and instead much of the night was spent in laughter. My husband was such a fun man who lived life on the edge. It was a wonder he made it forty-four years. Most of the stories revolved around danger, beer, and some kind of cool vehicle. I will cherish those stories forever.

As the night wore on and my exhaustion deepened, I asked Amy to get me a couple of Xanax. I knew I would not sleep without them. Conner asked if his friend Jackson, our cousin, could stay the night. I was relieved his parents said yes. Conner spent much of the evening distracted, running around outside with Jackson and other family and friends' children. Reality did not exist for Conner at that point. It had not settled into his bones and into his soul yet. His innocence was something for which I longed. His innocent laughter made me long for it myself. My poor, poor boy.

Once the Xanax kicked in, I told everyone I needed to go to bed. I thanked each of them for coming and told them how much Mike and I loved them. I hugged each guest as they filed past me on the way out. Our friends Erica and Jack, and their children, were the last to remain. Erica told my sister she would help me to bed. Erica walked with me to our bedroom and sat on the edge of the bed with me. She had a serious look on her face and said, "There's something I need to tell you."

I was confused and worried and asked, "What?"

"Mike visited Jack's dad."

"What do you mean?" I thought she meant Mike had visited Erica's father-in-law, Big Jack, one day before Mike passed away. Big Jack was battling cancer. I assumed she meant Mike had made it to their home in Eastwood one day recently, either before or after work. Mike had lost his dad in the same way Jack, Jr. was about to lose his. Cancer had robbed Mike's family of his dad, Bob, and now it was going to rob Jack, Jr.'s family of their dad. Mike would occasionally text Jack, Jr. and ask about his dad's progress, always hoping for the best but knowing the inevitable. Mike hated that his friend was dealing with the same thing as he had years ago.

"I mean Mike visited Jack."

I still didn't understand. Erica reached out and held my hand before continuing. "The day Mike died, Jack's dad had this weird look on his face like he was confused when we went out to tell him. He said, 'Yeah, I know. It was awful.'"

I frowned and shook my head, still not comprehending. Erica continued, "Jack asked who had called and told his dad, and his mom said no one. The phone hadn't been put back on the hook right, so it was busy all day long. No one could call in and there isn't cell phone service out there. No one had told them about Mike, but Big Jack said he knew Mike had been involved in a terrible accident at the concrete plant."

I shook my head still not fully grasping what she was trying to make me understand.

"No one told him. There's no way he could have known," Erica said.

"So, what are you saying? What do you think happened?"

"Mike visited Big Jack on his way to Heaven. He must have. There's no other explanation. We figure he stopped one last time to check on his friend's dad." Erica looked at me. "I can't tell you how much it means to Jack. All he can say is, 'I can't believe Mike was such a good friend to me that he stopped to check on my dad on his way to Heaven.'"

I bowed my head and squeezed her hand as I burst into tears, still shaking my head. Not in disbelief anymore, but in sorrow for the reality before me. I felt happy that Mike visited his friend's dad, but part of me felt a little jealous. I wished I had seen him one more time. I wished I had gone to him that day, surprised him with lunch, begged him to spend the day at home since I knew he did not feel well. But I was also grateful for my husband's heart. Mike's visit to Jack, Sr., only strengthened my belief that Mike had truly passed to Heaven.

"I think he did it to tell Jack's dad that whenever he's ready, Mike will be waiting for him, and everything will be okay," Erica said.

The hairs on my arms and neck rose. I hugged Erica and thanked her for telling me the story. I walked back into the living room with Erica and hugged Jack. He was ready to break down, so I just hugged him and told him thanks. I hugged each of their kids—Katie, Zach, and Tyler—and told them how much we loved them. They were the last to leave that night. Afterward, my sister walked Conner and me back to the bedroom.

Conner, Jackson, and I all slept in our king-sized bed, with Conner in the middle. I did not rest that night but felt thankful my little boy did. I was so grateful for Jackson being allowed to stay the night. It brought comfort and distraction to my poor broken son.

My husband was such an amazing man. It showed in the number of people who filed through the church, who formed the longest procession line of vehicles imaginable, and who created warmth on that lonely, cold night in our home.

We worked so hard to build this family. This family photo was taken during Fall of 2014, just months before Mike passed away.

The first time I visited the cemetery and Mike's USMC marker was placed, it took my breath away. It was placed before the main tombstone. I rub my hand along his name every time I visit the cemetery. I talk to him like he is there.

Conner is straightening the flag and flowers at Mike's grave. We chose a farm scene for the tombstone because he loved farming.

My wister (widow sister) and business partner Kimberly Homes. She and I launched our company Still His in early Spring of 2016. We met for the first time in Knoxville, Tennessee, where Alisha Bacon Photography took these photos.

Mike and Conner loved riding four wheelers around our farm and often Mike would stop and look around, just taking in all of the love and happiness he felt living here with us.

Mike's laugh was so contagious. His robust laugh and endearing smile lit up any room he walked into. It often radiated into people's hearts and souls. I loved his laugh and miss it so.

This was from the memorial shoot. Amanda was sure to place Mike above us, so that everyone knows we feel his presence and his absence every day, all at once. Amanda created this collage of sorts by shooting the barn and tree, us on the tailgate of Mike's truck, and then was able to insert his picture in the sky. He will always be a part of us.

Mike loved both his boys without end. This was his final Christmas. Only four days later he was gone.

We celebrated our ten-year anniversary in Las Vegas, Nevada, with our friends Jack and Erica Griffin.

Fourth of July was Mike's favorite holiday and was always spent with family.

Mike loved being a farmer. He would have done it the rest of forever, had he been given the chance.

Mike and his brother PR with their dad, Bob. Bob died of cancer when Mike was about twenty years old.

Mike showing a newborn Conner to our niece, Alyssa.

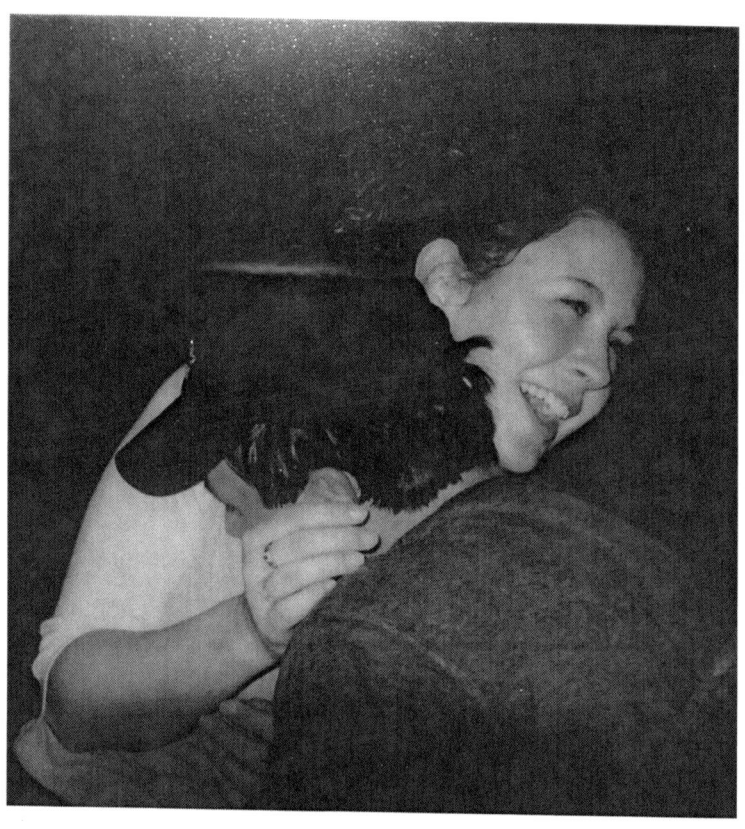

This was when we first began dating. We were so young and immediately in love.

Another tribute photo taken on the farm by Amanda Sly from Dazzle Photography.

This was on my birthday in July, 2014, just months before we lost Mike. We spent the weekend in Branson, Missouri, with both boys and felt so complete and happy.

Mike and Conner operating a backhoe at our old Garwood Farm. Conner wished he could spend every waking hour with his dad, his hero.

I was 23 and he was 31 in this photo taken at his grandma Holly's house in Van Buren. Mike's cousins were visiting from out of state and we were all going to the Current River to swim.

The boys taking a hunting break one deer season.

We often visited the minor league Springfield Cardinals games as a family.

Mike loved kids. He always made it fun for our boys and nephews every summer we had together.

Mike, our nephews, and sons, goofing off in the family pool at our rental house near our farm in Fremont. We moved there when I was seven months pregnant and spent Conner's first two years there.

Mike served two years in the US Marine Corps. I love this photo of him; he was so young and handsome. I did not know Mike during his Marine Corps days, but he spoke of his two years enlisted very fondly.

Conner as a penguin for his second Halloween.

Our family in Springfield, Missouri, when I was honored to sing the National Anthem for the Springfield Cardinals baseball team, a Minor League branch from the St Louis Cardinals.

Mike and his boys fishing at our old Garwood Farm pond.

Our last date a little more than a month before he passed away.

This was part of our first tribute photo session taken by a good friend, Amanda Sly with Dazzle Photography from Piedmont, Missouri. We moved to different locations on the farm and created photo books for family. We cherish these photos so much. Conner loves his dad's truck. He hopes to drive it when he turns sixteen.

This was Mike's childhood Bible that my mother-in-law, Chris, gave to us soon after Mike's passing.

For every birthday, we do a balloon release or a lantern release. We sing Happy Birthday to Mike and make his favorite cake, chocolate with chocolate icing.

My mom embracing me after the balloon release for Mike's 46th birthday, which was his second birthday spent in Heaven.

My mom, my sister Amy, and my father-in-law Gayle all support me as Mike's birthday balloons fly higher and higher.

Mike's second prom to attend with me over the years. I have always loved this picture of the two of us.

Another Marine Corps Mike. He was stationed at Twenty-Nine Palms.

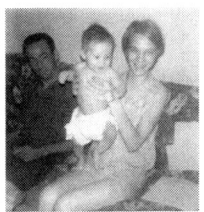
Mike as a baby with his dad Bob, and his mom Christine. Bob became ill with cancer when Mike was in The Marine Corps. Mike was about twenty when he lost his father.

Mike was born on the East Coast and moved to Missouri when he was about six.

Mike was so handsome, athletic, funny, and had tons of friends in school and adulthood.

Mike and his sweet momma Christine at Mike's high school graduation in 1989.

Mike was not big on bragging about his accomplishments, but in our community, big bucks were shown off.

This photo is from a summer camping trip one summer early in our relationship. Mike bought the small camper from his grandma Holly and we enjoyed it those first few summers together. Soon, life becamse too busy and Mike no longer had time to take us camping.

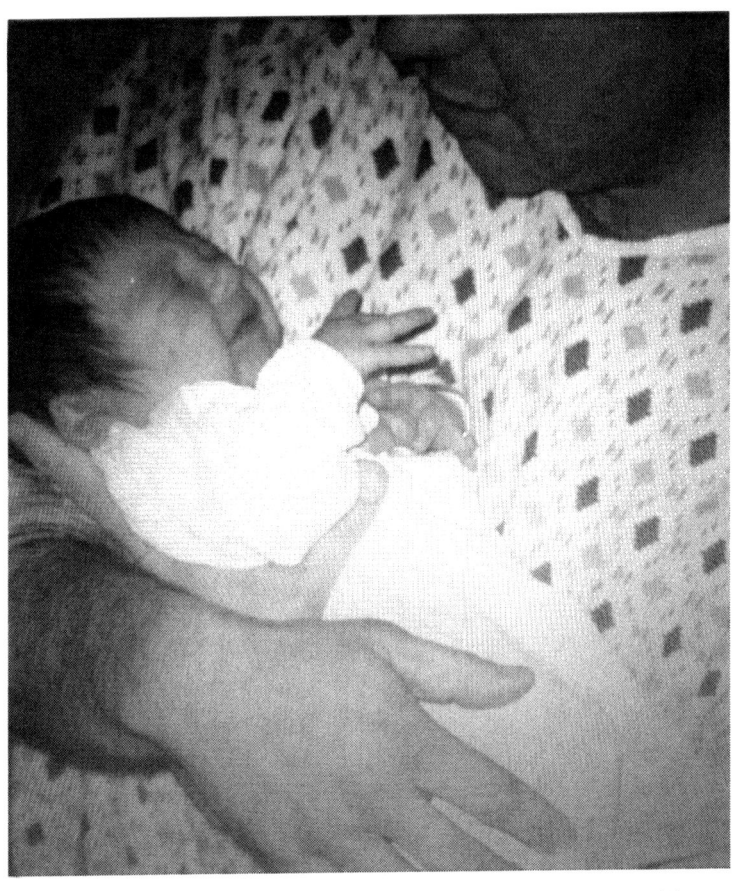

Mike swelled with pride when both of his sons came into this world.

Conner giving his daddy a hello kiss when we took Mike lunch one day. Mike was building fence at another piece of property so Conner and I would pack a picnic lunch as often as we could.

I had always wanted to be a mom, so when this day came, I was overfilled with joy and happiness and love. Mike was so proud.

Mike holding our niece, Reagan. She sure loved her Uncle Mike and he loved both of our nieces the same. He used to call them both "sweetie."

Mike and Conner when we lived in our rental property close to our Fremont farm. I love their matching flannels.

Mike, his brother PR, and sister Becky

August 9, 2003, in Eureka Springs, Arkansas, we were married.

A photo shoot by Amanda Sly of Dazzle Photography again, taken in early Fall 2017. It was like my "becoming the new me" shoot.

Mike and his boys having fun in the snow on our Fremont farm where we currently live.

Mike in his element for Fourth of July with his boys and our niece, Alyssa.

Mike and his sons during my birthday trip to Branson, the last family trip we would take.

Mike and his Grandma Mary, visiting at our annual Fourth of July Bash.

Mike, his stepdad Gayle, me and our brother-in-law Merlyn on a gigging Trip.

Our wedding day was perfect.

Life without Mike

Chapter Twelve

December 29, 2014, marked a catalyst for change in all parts of my life. Mike's death has affected change in my personality, my emotions, my actions, and my speech. It did the same for our son, Conner, who was only ten years old at the time of his dad's passing. Throughout my story of love, loss, and eventually hope, I have found that writing has been cathartic.

I have written personal journals, blogs, letters to Mike, letters from Mike as I imagined he would write them, and just general observations about life as a widow, a follower of Christ, and a solo mom. They all unfold upon these pages as they have come from the deepest parts of my heart and soul. My strength to begin pouring them onto paper did not begin until Mike was gone for four months.

And then writing became my therapy, my release, my place of refuge.

Mike's death became the beginning of a new me. Such tragedy takes a long time from which to heal. And healing is never complete, but rather a continuous process through which we must move at our own pace.

God is rooted in every step. God is rooted in every word. My heart is so broken still that even years later, my knees sometimes buckle, my breaths sometime become so labored I fear I'll pass out, my heartbeat speeds out of control, my hands shake, and I lose it. I cry. And cry . . . and cry . . . and cry . . . and I pray. I shout out to

God for help, for grace, for peace, for guidance. I ask Him to tell my husband how much we miss and love him.

The days are passing so quickly that I cannot fathom how time continues to march forward without Mike beside me. It has been years since I last heard his voice in the kitchen asking, "Do you want a cup of coffee, babe?" It has been years since he kissed me randomly, or wrapped his arms around me while we stood embraced, him leaning against the kitchen sink.

I don't understand how months, now years, have passed since we sent texts or called each other about work, the boys, or dinner plans. I can't believe it has been years since I looked into Mike's hazel eyes and knew he wanted me as badly as I wanted him. I can't believe my last phone call with my husband was about stupid cinnamon rolls.

There are so many things about life now, life without Mike that I do not understand or want to accept. So many "what ifs" and "I wish I hads." I don't have regrets about our marriage or what I would do differently in our love, but the *what if I had begged him to stay home that day . . .* or *I wish I had called him one more time to check on him that day* thoughts haunt me day and night.

It seems like only yesterday that I had him right here with me, loving me, talking to me, and sharing a life, a home, and a dream with me. He was mine and then I blinked and reality took it all away.

It feels like only seconds ago I was happy. I was safe and secure, sure of myself and of my husband. Now all of that is gone.

Sometimes I feel him talking to me. I feel his words pouring through my heart. Sometimes his words are so strong that they beg to be written. The first letter I really felt Mike wanted me to write was to Conner.

Dear Conner,

Hey buddy, Daddy sure misses you and loves you. I'm sorry I'm not there to be with you, son. I hope you know that Daddy never meant for any of this to happen. I still can't believe it myself. But I want you to know that I'm okay. I'm doing great and can see you all the way up here from Heaven. I get to talk to Grandpa Bob every day. We sit on a sunny hillside in the sunshine and talk and laugh all day long. He sure wishes he could have met you. Grandma Holly is up here too, and she loves watching all you do.

You know who else wishes he could have met you? Your Poppy Dave! He gets a kick out of you just as much as Grandma Holly does.

So, there are some things I want to tell you, son, that I won't be able to tell you in person. I know we had lots of talks before I left, but I worry you won't know what I wanted to tell you when you grow older.

First, always respect and listen to your mom. Daddy left her a big load and she is doing a good job trying to keep things together, but raising a rough little boy like you is tough for one momma to handle. She is your rock, son, and she always will be. She was mine, too. Respect her. Listen to her the FIRST time she says something. Don't argue or yell with her. Hug her lots every day because I miss being able to do that. She's the best momma you will ever have, so please treat her like she deserves to be treated.

Second, you've got a lot of work cut out for you. I sure do wish I had paid the farm off before I left so you could work on it without having to worry about payments, but I didn't have time to do that. So, it's going to be hard work. You're pretty young still so most of the work for now will be easy. Momma is going to have to do most of the big stuff, and she'll need some grown up help sometimes that you won't be able to do. But when you do get big enough, be ready to work hard.

Make Daddy proud. Take care of your cows. Take care of the hay and the fences and everything that comes with a farm. But if one day to decide you don't want it, you don't have to do it. I never forced your brother, so I won't force you. I hope one day you appreciate what I tried to build for you there but didn't get to finish. I hope you see the beauty in the life of a new baby calf and the smell of freshly cut hay.

I hope you realize my dream was to share that farm with you and your brother. To one day be retired and sit on the front deck with your mom and watch you on that tractor in the hayfield, working hard and making me proud. I sure do miss working with you. You have always been a hard worker.

Third, please keep doing well in school. I am so proud of you for sticking with it even when you have felt sad about me. I know it's been tough, buddy, but you have so many friends and your teachers and everybody have been real nice this year. You have stayed caught up with all your work and Momma told me about your last report card! All A's and one B+! That's so good, son. I'm proud of you. But remember, you have a lot more years, so keep at it. Remember when Daddy would tell you about some the grownups I had to teach who didn't do well in school? Well, it's a pain in butt, so you do well so you can go to college. You focus on those grades because you'll regret it one day if you don't.

Fourth, there's gonna be times when you get angry that I'm gone. I think you're probably gonna be mad at me, at Mom, at God, at whoever you can. Don't lose God, son, because I can tell you, even though I didn't go to church with you and Momma, I love God, and He loves me and you. Your faith in God, and especially the way you've kept that faith since this happened, is amazing to watch. I hear you pray every day. Sometimes it's at school, sometimes it's at home, and sometimes it's while driving in the truck. Keep praying. Keep believing. And keep going to church. Don't ever go against your beliefs and your faith, Bub. It's sometimes all you got.

Fifth, girls. Oh geez, did I have some stories I wanted to tell you when you get older. Momma wouldn't have liked some of them! Girls are awesome. But they are tricky too! Some of them are good and some are bad. As much as I hate to admit it, your mom is right; she is the one who needs to give you relationship advice. She was the best woman Daddy ever met. She is the kind of woman I told you that you need to find one day, but not one day soon.

Don't rush into anything with any girl, Conner, no matter how old you get. But if it feels right, and trust me, you'll know if it does, then go for it. Don't hold back and be afraid of getting hurt. If you fall in love like Daddy did with your momma, then you'll have butterflies in your stomach and you won't be able to quit grinning at the thought of her. You'll want to see her if even from a distance; you'll want to call her and hear her voice; you'll want to hold her hand and take her to your favorite places; you'll want to hold her tight and kiss her (I know, now you think it's gross, but when it's right and you're old enough, you won't); you'll want to build a life with her like Daddy did with Momma.

Don't ever hit a woman. Ever. Don't be mean to her and take your bad day out on her like I sometimes did with your mom. When you find the right one, she will be your rock. She needs to be the one you slow dance with in the kitchen. She needs to be the one you tell all your problems to. She needs to be the one you run to, not from. BUT make sure Momma likes her too. She will be the one who will kind of take the place of your mom in your life, so make it count. Make sure she respects your mom. Make sure she's a good one, son.

But another thing, don't let her run over you. Don't let her push you away or treat you badly. If she's a good woman, she won't, but I'm warning you, some women out there will try to hurt you or get you one way or another. Take your time to grow and have fun as a teenager and as a young man before you find "the one" and settle down.

Finally, never doubt for one second how much I loved you on Earth and love you still in Heaven. My gosh, the day you were born was one of the happiest days of my life. You and your brother were so important to me and still are. You two are the reason why I worked so hard. I wanted so badly to give you boys that farm one day. I wanted to see you two as partners. On the days you were born you both took my breath away. You were tiny and perfect and a gift to me and your mom. I could have sat and stared at you both for days. Shoot, I did lots of times.

You are creative and imaginative, Conner. You are good at art and at building things. I love you more than any words that have ever been invented. I would give anything to have not left you like I did. I hope you know that. I would have given anything to stay with you and to watch you grow and learn. I would have given anything to see you become a dad one day. I would give anything to hold you one more time, to hear "Watching You" or "He's Mine" again and listen to you sing it to me.

My heart doesn't break every day up here like yours does down there, because in Heaven there is no sadness or pain, no sickness, or anything bad. Daddy is happy. But that does not mean for one second that I forgot you or that I don't love you. You are still my world. You are still my little boy. You are still my best friend. So, talk to me. Every day, let me hear your voice. I don't get to talk back, but I bet you can guess what I would say.

Well, I have to go for now, buddy. Grandpa Bob has another story he wants to tell and I think Poppy Dave is gonna listen this time.

You take care of yourself, son, and of your mom, too. Can you hug her and kiss her for me, and tell her I love her too? Will you do the same for your brother? Tell him how proud I am of him too, and I can't believe he's about to graduate. Will you do that for me? I miss you all so much, but remember, I'm not sad. I'm not working today. I'm not lonely. And you know what else? I'm never leaving your heart. I'm right there in your memories. I'm in the sunshine and the spring flowers, I'm in the summer breezes and the cool river, I'm in the fall colors that grace the farm with beauty and in the call of the turkeys, and I'm in the white sparkles of the snow as it falls on our farm. I'm everywhere Bubby, and I will be with you forever.

I love you, Conner, now, forever, and always times infinity.
Love,
Daddy

Chapter Thirteen

GRIEF COMES IN WAVES. WE HAVE NO CONTROL OVER when it will wash over us and bring us crashing to our knees.

The love of my life, who always fixed any problem, who always made me feel safe, is gone. Forever. He's never coming back.

The weight of Mike's death becomes too heavy sometimes and the tears fall. I lose it. I can't lose control as often as I feel grief bubbling inside of me, since I have to stay strong for Conner. Sometimes it's too much. I don't feel strong. I want to cry and hide from the world. I want to grieve more, but I can't, because I'm expected to go to work, get dressed every day, and "move forward."

I envy any person's ability to bounce back from grief. I'm envious of their made-up faces and their bright eyes that don't look haggard and exhausted. I'm envious of their finances that allow them to travel the world. I'm envious of their positive outlook on life. Granted, I try my best to fulfill that same role. I apply the makeup, fix my hair, go to work and laugh. I now laugh often.

But many days, that isn't my reality. My reality is nowhere near beautiful, peaceful, happy, promising, or what I ever imagined it would be. My reality is harsh. I'm struggling. I have too many bills to pay. I have too much debt that surpasses my salary. I have sleepless nights. I worry about my son. I am lonely beyond any measure I have experienced before.

I know I'm not supposed to worry. I know I should give my worries to God, to lay them at His feet, and let His grace and mercy surround me and carry me. I know that. But it doesn't seem to help. I'm in a constant struggle about what I sincerely know, and the fear of the unknown.

I have an overwhelming fear of failure. Not simply a fear of farm-life failure, but also of failing to raise my son well. Of never finding true happiness again. I'm afraid I'll never be able to move forward without a wave knocking me to my knees. I fear I will never be loved like he loved me. I fear our son will never be "okay."

It seems like Mike could come home from work any minute. His truck still sits in its parking spot next to mine. His clothes hang in the closet, his razor and deodorant are still in his bathroom drawer. His office is full of his wastewater books and equipment. His smell is still lingering on the last pair of clothes that were in our hamper the day he left. His tools and equipment are in the barn. His coffee cups sit in the cabinet, yet I can't drink from them. His thermos sits in the cabinet. His boots are in the utility room. His rain jacket still hangs on the hook, and his Carhartt vest rests in the living room.

He is still here. But he is not. And that is terrible.

Chapter Fourteen

PEOPLE CHANGE. WE EVOLVE OVER TIME FROM OUR INFANT selves to our toddler selves, and on through to adulthood. That's a natural progression that often passes without many hiccups in the road.

Sometimes, God throws us hills and mountains on the journey, which make it difficult to step forward and to see the good in the present or on the other side. We are who we are before those mountains and hills, and then we are who we are after.

Before I met Mike, I was a young, divorced, insecure twenty-three-year old. The divorce changed me.

I have always lacked confidence with my appearance. I have always feared my partner would not like me anymore and leave me for someone else. In my younger years, I was jealous, worried, and often hateful as a defense to those fears. After my divorce, I realized it wasn't only my ex's fault. Yes, he did wrong, but so did I. I was too young when we married, and we had been a couple since the summer I turned thirteen. I think we outgrew each other. But nonetheless, our divorce changed me.

After our divorce, I became even more worried than before. If my own husband didn't want me, I thought no other man would. I thought I would die alone. So, for a few months I wallowed in self-pity. Until one day I had an epiphany: I was not going to die alone.

I stood in my rental house bathroom and gazed at myself in the mirror. I realized that I might not be Cindy Crawford, but I wasn't ugly, either. I would eventually be okay and if someone were to call and ask me out, I would go. I forgave my ex-husband and eventually forgave myself.

Mike became that someone. He called me one October evening and changed my life forever. For the better.

I was in love with his voice from the first, "Hey . . . " I fell in love with him within a week, and he fell in love with me. He said, "I love you" first, thank God, because I thought he would think I was insane for falling in love so fast.

Mike changed me. Before him, I felt worried no one would want me; that I would never find true happiness and real, grown-up love, rather than the high school kind. Before Mike, I never wanted to dress sexy; I always feared I would look stupid or fat in sexy clothes, and that it would be a turn off for any man. He built my confidence.

Before Mike, I had no real dreams for a future. Sure, my ex and I had talked about what it would be like when we were old, but I don't think either of us really believed it or meant it. We only fantasized about it, and we were too young to fully commit to a life together.

Mike and I did, though. We had a dream together and we worked for it every day. We lived that beautiful dream for thirteen years, two months, and eleven days, and it changed me for the better.

I had never trusted anyone like I trusted Mike. I had never believed in someone like I believed in Mike. I had never cheered for someone so hard, never wanted someone so badly, and never loved someone so fully.

Mike made me feel like a whole new woman because he made me feel beautiful even when I looked like crap. No makeup, disheveled hair . . . it didn't matter. He found me my most beautiful when I was dressed in my torn farm jeans, boots, and one of his flannel shirts. Makeup free, hair flying wild.

He had eyes that pierced my soul with every smoldering look. He looked at me with pure love, what we called "our forever look."

We were in it together, forever. It didn't matter what hills and mountains came our way; we were determined to make it to the other side, unscathed.

And when Mike looked with pure love and happiness and pride at his sons, I'd fall even deeper in love with him.

Before Mike, I was unsure of my future; and when we met and fell in love with each other, I was less insecure. I was sure we'd make it all the way to sitting on the porch after retirement, watching our boys with their families. Watching our grandkids play in the yard. Taking in each other in the quiet moments alone.

I was safe with Mike. No matter what, life was good.

And now. What a difference. What about now? My life will never be the same and neither will my son's. My heart will never fully heal. My love will never fade for Mike or for the life we shared for so many years.

After Mike died . . . That's difficult to accept as reality. To move forward from the *after* terrifies me.

Now, I'm a nervous wreck, back to my insecure self. I worry I'll fail as a single mom. I worry day and night about my abilities as a solo parent. Our son has suffered from anxiety his entire life, and now without his dad, it has intensified.

I worry that I'll worry forever. I feel like I'm spinning in circles inside my mind, inside my emotions. Butterflies stir day and night.

Some days, I grit my teeth most hours of the day to keep my cool, and sometimes I'm too weak and it breaks me. But I'm trying for our son. Every day is a struggle that takes a conscious effort to *not* lose control. I have to will myself to smile, to laugh, to take steps forward.

I'm doing what I know would make Mike happy. I knew him better than anyone. We shared secrets and conversations no one else was privy to. We told each other things we dared not say aloud to anyone else. We were each other's forever.

So now I smile, years after Mike died, mostly to fight the sadness. I smile in spite of the fears. I place my feet, one in front of the other, in spite of the worries. Some days I fake being happy, secure, and sure. I fake self-confidence. In reality, underneath the mask, I'm scared to death. I'm overwhelmed with the farm, house, and to-do lists. I am overwhelmed with raising a teenage boy without his dad. I cry at night, in the silence while Conner sleeps, so he won't hear me.

Chapter Fifteen

About five months after Mike's passing, Conner and I took our first vacation without Daddy. It was a bittersweet moment for us; Conner's eleventh birthday, and his first trip to the ocean and the beach.

We traveled with my mom, my sister and her family, and an aunt and uncle, to St. George Island, Florida. I had been to the beach before, but Conner had not. I was never able to convince Mike to take a beach vacation, and shortly after he passed away, I vowed to our son to take him on at least one vacation per year, finances allowing.

St. George Island, Florida, is a small island community unscathed by commercialism. Locally owned restaurants fill the center of the community and vacation homes stretch for miles on the beach. Groceries must be purchased almost an hour away and there are no amusement parks or shopping malls.

While I did my absolute best to make the vacation special, I wept every day for the absence of my husband.

Every morning, I snuck out to the beach before Conner awoke, and I watched the ocean waves in silence. I wanted to sit in solitude, take in the waves and the wind, and do nothing but cry. In the evenings, as the sun set in the horizon, producing the magical twilight hour on the waves, I would sit alone with my thoughts of Mike, or of Conner's and my futures. I usually waited until everyone was in bed, or at least tried to wait until it was just my mom and me on the beach to cry the gut-wrenching sobs to which I have grown accustomed.

I embarrassed myself one day when I broke down in the middle of a crowded beach restaurant. Families were everywhere, laughing, building happy memories. Our family sat at a table against one wall, facing the ocean. We all ordered drinks and a beautiful spread of fresh seafood adorned the table. As I watched husbands with their wives, dads with their children, my throat constricted. I had to quickly excuse myself and make my way outside where I sat alone and cried.

Conner met me outside after he bought me some earrings, which I didn't know about. He has become very good at surprising, just like his dad used to, with those Mike Hollis' smooth moves. I hugged Conner and cried into his chest. He held me close and told me just like he had the day his dad died, "It will be all right, Momma. I love you."

While we were at this beautiful beach destination, I kept thinking it was more of a couples' place to visit. It was nice for families, but so quiet and peaceful that Conner grew bored.

I imagined what Mike and I would have done together if we had been there as a couple. I imagined us walking along the sand under the moonlit sky, with stars shining above us. I imagined walking around in downtown Apalachicola, Mike's hand folded into mine and his left hand leading me into a nice restaurant. I imagined us going for pizza and beer. I dreamed of us relaxing in the beach chairs with the breeze blowing and the sun kissing our skin. I imagined us going inside the house after a long day on the beach, napping for long enough to get our energy back up for a date. I imagined listening to the live band playing as Mike looked at me like I was the most beautiful woman on Earth. I imagined Mike and me talking and laughing and spending quality time together, falling in love all over again.

It was difficult to be there without him. It didn't matter that I was surrounded by loving family. It didn't matter that the beach was full; I felt alone. It didn't matter that I laughed out loud . . . most of the laughs were only to keep the tears away.

I thought of Mike often while driving the fourteen hours there and back. I remembered so many romantic things about him.

I imagined the times I sat close to him with my hand on his right leg while he rested his chin on his left hand and steered with his right. I imagined Conner on the Ranger behind or in front of us . . . how Mike grinned at how much Conner had grown and how much of a little "man child" he had become. The warmth of his body as I sat close to him, both of us dressed in faded jeans and flannel shirts. The look he would shoot over to me as he told me I was beautiful and that he loved me. The way he stole a few kisses here and there and Conner rolled his eyes and shook his head when he caught us. Old country music on the radio as I sang along, us jamming out when a good old favorite came on, like "Baby Got Her Blue Jeans On."

So, our first vacation, as with every other vacation since, contained a mixture of emotions. They take effort on both our parts to enjoy. Each new one is plagued by Mike's absence and our longing to have him back.

I made memories with our little boy while we were on vacation, but he struggled too. He missed his dad building sandcastles with him. He missed hearing his dad's laughter and seeing his smile. And, it was the week of Conner's eleventh birthday. His first without his dad.

Chapter Sixteen

I REMEMBER THE FIRST TIME MIKE LEFT ME SURPRISE POST-IT notes trailing to the bedroom. I arrived home to the old Garwood farm one evening after work, and Mike had actually beaten me home that night. I walked up to our deck, drained from the day's work, to find a yellow Post-it note on the sliding glass door with, "Come inside and meet me in the bedroom," written on it. Post-it notes trailed all the way to the bedroom with compliments and reasons why he loved me and wanted me.

Mike pulled off the first surprise when we first started dating. Mike worked with a couple of friends on a water system one day and he planned to work late into the night. I arrived home from teaching in Mountain View, showered, and settled in for the night in my bathrobe, one of those fluffy, granny gowns.

Mike called to say goodnight around ten-thirty p.m. During our conversation, I heard a knock at my front door.

"Babe, someone just knocked on my door! It's almost eleven, who in the world would be coming over this late?" I was scared to answer my door.

Mike reassured me he would not hang up until we knew who was knocking on my door.

"It's okay, I'm not going anywhere, just go open the door and stay on the line. Do not hang up the phone," he said sternly, sounding as worried as me.

I tiptoed to my living room, breathing heavily from fear, and slowly opened the door with the phone still held to my ear.

Mike stood on my front porch, with his phone in one hand, and a pizza and six-pack of beer in the other. He smiled that perfect smile.

Our last date took place only weeks before he left us. I made a romantic playlist, consisting of Ed Sheeran, Blake Shelton, and several others. Mike listened to me sing along to them as a serenade to him, while he held my hand and grinned from the driver's seat of my truck. We went to dinner and a movie, but we didn't make it to the end. Conner was with Grandma Jackie, my mom, so we left early for more time together.

I remember how my husband flirted with me every day; he complimented me a million times a day; he held me. He'd come up behind me and kiss my neck, and tell me he loved me. He was the absolute strongest, toughest, most hardworking man I've ever known, but he was also the sweetest, most romantic man I've ever known.

I have a note which I carried in my wallet for eleven years. After he passed, I laminated it and placed it in the safe deposit box.

Mike left the note for me one morning when he left for work before I woke. It reads: "Hey babe, just wanted to tell you that I love you and the baby." I was a few months pregnant with our son. Very few people knew he was such a romantic.

Conner's and my routines changed immediately with Mike's death. When evening falls and it approaches six or seven p.m. in the "normal" world, some families are settling in for the night to have dinner, watch TV, and talk about their days. At least that's what my family did before we lost Mike.

I'm baffled at not having a routine anymore. I don't know how to establish new routines for Conner and myself. I want to sit on the porch and watch the cows like we used to, but the chair beside me is empty. I want to hop in an old farm truck and take a ride around the farm, but I don't want to be the one driving. I want to talk. Talk about nothing and everything. But I find myself sitting in silence. Tears come before I go back inside and I need to clench my jaw again.

My cooking routine is also completely out of whack. I don't cook much anymore, and when I do, there is way too much food. I have not mastered the art of cooking for two. Mike loved my cooking and I loved cooking for him. He liked everything, except one time I tried a new recipe for chicken enchiladas and they came out green. We did not eat those!

My laundry routine is different. I used to get so aggravated at the pile of grease, concrete and cow manure-stained pants, but I would give anything to have those in the hamper again.

I just do not know how to start new routines when I'm still stuck in the old ones, desperately wishing for them to return. Part of our routine is to visit Mike in the cemetery. I hate that our visits are one-sided. I hate that his name is in stone. I hate that this happened to him; to us.

How do I start new routines that aren't heartbreaking? All too often my attempt to establish a new routine for my son and me ends in a fit of anger. My sleep pattern has no routine now, unless one could say the absolute lack of sleep is a routine.

My work alarm wakes me around five-thirty a.m., but often I will wake earlier, usually by four a.m. My mind won't shut up. Usually my thoughts travel to what I miss about Mike.

After all, he was mine.

He was just here.

He loved me, really and truly loved me.

He held my hand.

He kissed me often.

He told me how much he loved me every day.

He fought with me.

He made up with me.

He whispered sweet nothings and secret longings in my ear.

He looked at me.

He looked into my soul.

He held me up when I felt weak.

He took care of me when I was sick.

He laughed so hard with me.

He made me laugh so hard with him.

He made love to me like I was the only woman he had ever been with.

He made me feel special.

He actually made me feel beautiful, which has always been a difficult task.

He made me trust fully.

He made me believe in happiness again.

He sang when he thought I couldn't hear.

He watched me when I didn't know he was looking.

He surprised me.

He left me notes.

He took me on adventures.

He taught me how to farm. I'm still working on that.

He got angry at his cows and threw little fits that I miss.

He taught me how to drive a tractor.

He smiled when he saw me driving his truck.

He taught me how to tear down my walls.

He taught me how to fight for what I want.

He listened to me and what upset me. It took him a few years to learn that one.

He swept me off my feet.

He stole my heart, my mind, my body, and my soul within a few days.

He asked me to marry him at a roadside park.

He promised his love and life to me on an August evening.

He was proud to be seen with me.

He grew to like kissing me in public . . . not raunchy kissing . . . just a simple, perfect kiss.

He complimented me multiple times every single day.

He blessed me with a son.

He held our son and placed him in my arms.

He rocked our son to sleep at night when I needed a turn to rest.

He slow danced in the living room with our baby in his arms.

He slow danced with me in the kitchen.

He filled my life with small, perfect, simple memories.

He cried.

He cried because his oldest son didn't live with us.

He cried when his oldest son didn't come over for the weekend.

He cried when plans changed in the blink of an eye, without warning.

He cried at people's evilness.

He cried out of guilt.

He made mistakes that to some were unforgivable.

He was afraid to forgive himself for the way his first marriage ended.

He never did.

He was insecure.

He felt he was never good enough, though he was beyond any measure of "good enough."

He was selfless.

He helped his friends any time they called.

He worked harder than any man I've ever known.

He never stopped working.

He fought me over work.

He took on too much.

He could never stop; he didn't have a choice.

He died while working.

He left us.

He didn't mean to.

He is still my husband.

I am still his wife.

His boys are still his sons.

Chris is still his mom.

Becky is still his sister.

P.R. is still his brother.

My family is still his family.

My heart is still his.

My soul still belongs to him.

My heart still breaks every day.

My soul still aches every second.

My son cries for his dad almost every day.

We both have dreams of Mike.

We both toss and turn and are restless when we do sleep.

I worry.

I can't control it.

I break down at random moments and sometimes in the most random places.

I can't control that either.

One evening on the vacation to St. George Island with our boy, I felt like I just had to share the experience with Mike:

Babe,

Today we are celebrating our boy's eleventh birthday. I feel lost.

I brought Conner to the beach; Mom, Amy, and everyone is here with us. We have come to St. George Island, Florida, surrounded by our family. But I feel utterly alone and it is taking every ounce of my being to refrain from cracking. The first morning here, I walked to the beach alone. I sat on the damp, cool morning sand with a hot cup of coffee in hand. Merlyn joined me and put his arm around me. I cried on his shoulder, wishing so much that you were here with us.

Conner awoke to the waves this morning and he has been doing well so far. He cried once a little, and so he and I rested under the shade of the canopy for a bit. We whispered about you. He misses you so much. I hate so much that his birthdays from now on are all tainted with grief.

I'm trying to stay upbeat and laugh my hardest, and smile my widest, all while barely hanging on. I feel like I could sit on this beach in silence, with only the waves crashing in front of me. I want to hold our boy close to me, and stare into the power before us.

I remember the day he was born, don't you? It seems like it was yesterday that we went to the hospital to be induced. Remember how we didn't decide on a middle name until the morning we left for the hospital? We decided that day to honor my Poppy Dave, my mom's dad. Conner now has Poppy Dave's middle name, and I love the name Luin. Conner Luin is a great name, but now more than ever I wish we had given him Michael as a middle name.

I don't know how I am supposed to celebrate all of his birthdays without you. Planning what gifts to buy him or what food to serve at the party has always been a team effort. Watching you smile and laugh and relax at his parties brought me such joy. You actually took off work for both boys' birthdays. I miss the way you would come up behind me, kiss me on the shoulder, and say, "Hey babe, you did good. I think he's having fun, don't you?"

This year he didn't even want a party. He didn't want a dinner or any celebration with family and friends because he said it would remind him that you're not here.

Everything reminds us that you are not here. Even though we've never been to this place with you, and there is no memory here of us, I feel weird being here with my family when the biggest part of my family is gone. I feel completely lonely even though we're surrounded by people who love us. I miss you and I know your little boy does, too.

I find myself wishing I could curl up next to you on a beach and close my eyes and take in the sound of the waves and the warmth of the sun while I find myself stopping every so often during the day to tell you how much I miss you.

I search in my mind for moments full of you. During everything we've done here at the beach, I imagine the same situations and experiences but with my husband. My best friend, my true love. The best memories of my life have been made with you. I wish you were here to make memories with our little boy and me on his first trip to the ocean.

Part of it is beautiful in that I still think of you in everything I do; but part of it is gut wrenching. Part of me is gone. Part of me will never heal. Part of me will crack and not be able to hold on anymore. That part came out at dinner, in a crowded beach restaurant, with our table filled with our family. There was no stopping it. I held it in for as long as I could. I had to excuse myself from the restaurant and cry alone in the parking lot. A restaurant full of happy families ripped my heart into pieces.

I cannot wait until we can all reunite in Heaven one day and have the biggest birthday party for all those who will be missed here on Earth.

I have to go for now, as our amazing son is calling me back to the waves. I love you and miss you now, forever, and always times infinity, babe.

Chapter Seventeen

SOME DAYS I SEE MY HUSBAND EVERYWHERE. RECENTLY, I found a picture of me that Mike had taken early on in our relationship. I was lying on the couch with my legs tucked up wearing one of his denim button-up shirts. It reminded me of how excited we made each other from day one, and this excitement continued for thirteen years.

In February 2002, only four months into our relationship, I moved in with Mike. He was elated. We spent days and nights together on that original Garwood farm, in that small single-wide trailer. It was perfect and it became our home. We had so much fun.

One of my favorite memories of our time in Garwood is when we shared a twelve-pack of Bud Light and spray-painted one of his old farm trucks camouflage. We played Mike's Creedence Clearwater Revival CD, laughed, flirted, and spray painted each other a little, too. The truck was parked under two huge shade trees in front of the barn. The sun was shining, and I wore my cut-off denim shorts, a T-shirt, and sandals. Mike wore his usual attire of Carhartt jeans, T-shirt and boots.

Other favorite memories include the times we rode through the farm, stopped on a hillside, and made out, just kissing and holding each other, watching the cows. We looked up at the stars, talked, and shared our dreams.

Mike loved me and wanted me even when I thought I looked gross. I was young and in the best shape of my life, but my confidence still lacked. Mike tried to build my confidence. He would leave me notes trailing to the bedroom. He would run me a bubble bath and take me by the hand to lead me to the bathtub. He never stopped trying to make me understand that he thought I was the most beautiful woman in the world.

Another favorite memory is the first night we brought Conner home. I was in pain and exhausted. Conner seemed to wake up constantly wanting to nurse, and I begged Mike to take Conner for fifteen minutes to let me rest. It lasted all of three minutes because I couldn't lie there without my baby boy, so he brought him back to me and I cradled him in my arms.

I remember the night we sat at the kitchen table and decided on our son's middle name. I remember Conner's first Easter egg hunt and how exciting it was when he found his first egg. I remember Conner's first sled ride when Daddy sat our baby boy into the sled and pulled him around.

I remembered riding with him to check on the cows and feed them. Mike would stop the truck, look over God's beauty stretched out before us, and then look at me. He'd tell me how beautiful I was no matter if I wore a hat and no makeup, or if I had just changed clothes from church, with makeup and fixed hair.

I am tired of only "seeing" my husband without having him. I am tired of being sad he isn't here. I am tired of not sleeping. I am tired of the dreams that make my stomach hurt. I can't breathe when it hits me. The waves wash over me with no warning.

I am tired of sleeping on Mike's side of the bed and Conner sleeping on the side that used to be mine. I am tired of seeing Mike's last work clothes packed into a bag in the closet. I am tired of not hearing his voice. I am tired of trying to keep my crap together. I am tired of working so hard on this farm. I am tired of feeling guilty because I didn't work as hard on the farm while he was here. I am tired of being angry. I am tired of being sad. I am tired of being a widow.

I want my husband back and I want our dreams back. I want to sit in the field with him and watch the cows, hold his hand, and spend an hour doing nothing but kissing. I want to lie beside him in our bed. I want to find notes that start on the sliding glass door and lead me to him. I want to laugh with him and cry with him, share secrets with him and dreams with him. I want my life back.

I know it can't happen, but I'm not ready to accept that yet.

Michael,

I miss that one of your hazel eyes was a little greener than the other.

I miss the rough callouses on your hands but the gentle way you used them with me.

I loved that our names became "babe" or "baby" after about the first week of dating.

I loved that we didn't have only one song, but so many.

I miss the way I could walk into your office and see you sitting at your desk; I'd walk over to your chair and you'd put your arm around my waist and look up to kiss me.

I miss that when it rained, you would come home and rest, or sometimes change into dry clothes and take us back out with you.

I loved that I never felt afraid with you.

I never doubted what my future would be like; I never felt nervous about lawyers because I didn't need them for anything; I never worried about bills.

I miss the way you would read a book a gazillion times instead of spending five dollars on a new one.

I miss the way you would surprise me with little gifts.

I miss the time Conner and I went with you to the lake for a week while you were teaching and you came to the hotel to get us for dinner. Jason Aldean had just released "Big Green Tractor," and I loved that song. You always told me how much it reminded you of us. So, Conner and I got in the truck to go to dinner with you and that song began playing. I, of course, turned it up louder and sang along, smiling and looking at you with your perfect smile. After it ended I said, "I love that song," and turned the radio down. A new song began and it sounded like Jason Aldean again. So, I was like, "Hmmm they must be doing one of those back to back things because I swear that's him again." You smiled. When the third song came on, I connected the dots. You surprised me with the CD and had it ready on the song for me.

I miss so much about you that I couldn't sleep last night.

I miss the raspy tone in your voice, especially when it was just the two of us.

I miss the secrets we used to share that no one else knew.

I loved that you put your guard down in front of me and cried when you needed to.

I miss the way you would yell, "Babe, what is wrong with you?" when I would put my cold feet on you at night.

Or when I was hot flashing and you would look at me and say, "Yeah I know you're hot . . ." with a wicked grin.

I miss dressing up for you; I wanted to look perfect for you, or as best as I could.

I love that you always told me, "Thanks for still trying for me, babe . . ." and you would tell me I was beautiful.

I miss when you would come into the bathroom while I was getting ready for work and talk to me, usually coming up behind me, just staring, and then kissing my neck, telling me how beautiful you thought I was.

I miss that you would tell me over and over again over the years how much we were made for each other; how we were a perfect fit in so many ways.

I miss your stare . . . you'd stare at me randomly for no reason. I would ask, "What?"

I miss how you used to have to write things down or you'd forget; after you left I found a sticky note in your desk labeled: "August 9, 11 years."

I miss the way when we first began you would still write your to-do list in military time.

I miss the way I would have to tell you to slow down when eating because I wasn't your drill sergeant and wasn't going to make you drop and give me twenty.

I miss your walk; you had a very confident walk.

I miss when you would tell me that you loved to watch me walk away.

I love that you kept all of the pictures Conner drew for you and would tape them up anywhere; they are still taped to your office wall and office door.

I love that you were so proud of our family and what we had built together. You would randomly pull over to a hilltop and we would sit and watch the cows and you would say, "I know our life isn't easy, babe, I know that, but I know I wouldn't want to be anywhere else, doing anything else, with anyone else. I think we have a good life and I think we sure are lucky and blessed."

Yeah, we sure were lucky and blessed.

I loved it all.

Now, let me tell you what I hate.

I hate that we didn't spend more time together, even though in the beginning we said we needed to still be husband and wife and not just become Mom and Dad.

I hate that we didn't take more family vacations with the boys.

I hate that you worked too much and we fought about it.

I hate that we fought about money, and how you spent too much on building your dream.

I hate that I didn't get a second job to try and make more money to help you finance your dream.

I hate that our boys lost their dad.

I hate that you won't be there for their weddings.

I hate that you won't get to hold your grandchildren.

I hate that I sleep without you.

I hate that I crave someone beside me; I miss the way we would sit beside each other, my legs draped onto your lap and your hands resting on my legs.

I hate that I cry so much.

I hate the sick feeling in my stomach.

I hate that I don't get to hear your voice unless I play the recording on my phone.

I hate that every single picture brings back a story.

I am happy and love that we have so many stories but I hate that all they are now are memories and I can't build any more with you.

I hate that you have a grave I visit less often than I wish I could.

I hate that there is a stone with your name carved into it.

I hate the way you died; that is something I cannot put out of my mind.

I hate that my heart breaks all over again every morning when I wake, like it's the first day without you.

I hate that my friends feel sorry for me.

I hate that my family feels sorry for me.

I hate that people have expectations and I don't want to meet any of them.

I hate that any move I make will probably be judged by others, even though I do not care at all because my inner judge knows what I'm doing is right.

I hate that Conner and I are alone most of the time.

I hate that you left me; you left us.

I hate that we promised now, forever, and always times infinity, and here I am left alone to finish it.

I hate that we didn't meet each other earlier in life.

I hate that we only got thirteen years, two months, and eleven days to be together.

I hate that you didn't stop at my apartment sooner to ask me out.

I hate that I didn't go riding with you on the farm, or to the treatment plants, or wherever, every time you asked.

I hate that I used to get angry about your cow-manure stained pants; I'd give anything to wash them again.

I hate that I can only smell you on the last outfit you had in the hamper and on your Carhartt coat I have sealed in a bag.

I hate that there is still so much to sort through and I can't even touch half of it in your office; I can't make myself do it.

I hate the endless depth of loneliness I feel without you.

I hate the void that will never be filled in your boys' lives.

You should still be here.

That was our deal.

Now, forever, and always times infinity . . . remember?

how much it reminded you of us. So, Conner and I got in the truck to go to dinner with you and that song began playing. I, of course, turned it up louder and sang along, smiling and looking at you with your perfect smile. After it ended I said, "I love that song," and turned the radio down. A new song began and it sounded like Jason Aldean again. So, I was like, "Hmmm they must be doing one of those back to back things because I swear that's him again." You smiled. When the third song came on, I connected the dots. You surprised me with the CD and had it ready on the song for me.

I miss so much about you that I couldn't sleep last night.

I miss the raspy tone in your voice, especially when it was just the two of us.

I miss the secrets we used to share that no one else knew.

I loved that you put your guard down in front of me and cried when you needed to.

I miss the way you would yell, "Babe, what is wrong with you?" when I would put my cold feet on you at night.

Or when I was hot flashing and you would look at me and say, "Yeah I know you're hot . . ." with a wicked grin.

I miss dressing up for you; I wanted to look perfect for you, or as best as I could.

I love that you always told me, "Thanks for still trying for me, babe . . ." and you would tell me I was beautiful.

I miss when you would come into the bathroom while I was getting ready for work and talk to me, usually coming up behind me, just staring, and then kissing my neck, telling me how beautiful you thought I was.

I miss that you would tell me over and over again over the years how much we were made for each other; how we were a perfect fit in so many ways.

I miss your stare . . . you'd stare at me randomly for no reason. I would ask, "What?"

I miss how you used to have to write things down or you'd forget; after you left I found a sticky note in your desk labeled: "August 9, 11 years."

I miss the way when we first began you would still write your to-do list in military time.

I miss the way I would have to tell you to slow down when eating because I wasn't your drill sergeant and wasn't going to make you drop and give me twenty.

I miss your walk; you had a very confident walk.

I miss when you would tell me that you loved to watch me walk away.

I love that you kept all of the pictures Conner drew for you and would tape them up anywhere; they are still taped to your office wall and office door.

I love that you were so proud of our family and what we had built together. You would randomly pull over to a hilltop and we would sit and watch the cows and you would say, "I know our life isn't easy, babe, I know that, but I know I wouldn't want to be anywhere else, doing anything else, with anyone else. I think we have a good life and I think we sure are lucky and blessed."

Yeah, we sure were lucky and blessed.

I loved it all.

Now, let me tell you what I hate.

I hate that we didn't spend more time together, even though in the beginning we said we needed to still be husband and wife and not just become Mom and Dad.

I hate that we didn't take more family vacations with the boys.

We said it all the time.

We meant it.

I hate that our deal is broken.

Not on purpose, I know, but still it has been broken.

I just miss you. And I miss us.

I miss happiness.

Chapter Eighteen

CHILD REARING IS STRENUOUS, TO SAY THE LEAST. CHILD rearing as a solo parent is like nothing I have ever known. Grieving children make the task feel near impossible. Conner was ten years old when he lost his dad. Right on the cusp of those impressionable years, Conner's brain was unable to accept or process his dad's death. Now we are in the teen years and it has often felt like the apocalypse inside our house. My child has cried, yelled, broken things, punched pillows, and gone through every emotion imaginable.

One evening, after a particularly powerful outburst, Conner and I sat on the front deck and had a much-needed talk. My child is a strong-willed, stubborn, smart-mouthed kid. He was that way before we lost Mike, and he has since increased his eye-rolling, stomping off, arguing, and attitude. I find myself raising my voice way too often.

He has seen multiple counselors and tried journaling and drawing through his grief.

I'm exhausted mentally, emotionally, and physically. We both are. I don't have the energy to fight one more fight, especially not with my child. So, we have had serious life discussions. I cry. He cries. And I hope it affects him like I intend.

Here is what I usually tell him, or something alone these lines:

"Conner, we've got to fix us. We've always been close and anyone can see that. But son, since Daddy has been gone you have disrespected me more often than you did before. I don't have your dad to hold over you anymore. I can't say, 'Be good, or I'm telling your dad.' I can't say, 'Look, Mom needs a break and a little bit of Mom time, so you need to go spend the day with your dad today.'

"Your attitude needs help, and I have a plan to help us both. I want to help you realize what we are here for and I want to help myself make better days for us both. Let me tell you what I have. Conner, I have finally understood and accepted that Daddy received the *gift* of going to Heaven. He wasn't taken from us because we did anything bad. He *got* to leave this place. He gets to rest all day; he doesn't have to work; he isn't sick; he isn't even worried about us. He doesn't know how sad we are. Daddy is okay. He is happy.

"But you know what else I realized? Just like your dad received the *gift* of Heaven, we received the gift of a life continued. We *get* to stay here and live, Conner, and that's what we need to do. The other day I wrote to your dad and told him I hope his feet are planted firmly on Heaven's ground when I get to Heaven, because I'll come running when it's my turn.

"I can't wait to see him and to get to be with him. And I can't. But you know what I want to be able to do when I get there? I want to tell Daddy all the good stuff we did when he left. I want to tell Daddy that when he died, *we* didn't. We didn't sit here and fall apart. I don't want to tell him that when he left, you turned on me, Conner. I don't want to tell him that we died when he did and sat here feeling miserable. Daddy would feel guilty if I told him that.

"I want to tell Daddy that I raised you well after he left. I want to tell Daddy that we did well together, and we made it. I want to tell him that we lived so we can tell him as much good stuff as we can when we get there.

"Conner, I can't do this on my own. I can't argue with you and let you disrespect me. I want us to be happy and fill the days with things we can tell Daddy. I want to be happy again. We have who knows how long left on this earth to live, to make memories, to make choices that will help us tell Daddy either good stuff or bad stuff. Which would you rather tell him?"

I sometimes feel like I have talked until I am blue in the face. Or that I am talking to a brick wall. After all, Conner is Mike Hollis' son.

But, I keep at it, as we all do. I keep at it because I need to build a life for my son and me that will make my husband proud and happy, not regretful and sorrowful. I can't build memories if we are fighting all the time. I know that Conner is angry. I am angry, too. We both have much to be angry about. We lost the center of our world. Our lives came to a screeching halt in the middle of a December day, and nothing has since or ever will be the same. But that does not mean it is okay for us to veer off course and stop living a good life. I want to tell my husband how much we have continued to love him and have honored his memory through the good things in our lives.

I can't wait to get to Heaven to see my husband. I can't wait to wrap my arms around his neck and kiss his face until I can't kiss it anymore. I can't wait to tell him how well his little boy and I lived for him so we could share our stories of happiness and success, of dreams and realities.

Every day brings some level of struggle. I still grit my teeth; I still cry a little bit every day; I still dream of the man I am so deeply in love with; I still hear his voice and miss his touch; I still suffer through so much pain in silence to protect my child. But I cannot die emotionally. I cannot quit. Mike would not want me to. He won't let me quit. Some days I want to, trust me! The desire to throw my hands in the air and walk away tugs at my soul. But I won't quit. No, I am most certainly not suicidal; I just mean to quit *this* life. To run away. To start anew.

So, I will live my life the best I know how until I see my husband again. I will raise our son with as much respect and faith as I can so hopefully we end up with a young man who is respected, respectful, and loved, who is kind and selfless, and who is a hard worker and a loving man. I will not quit, and I am hopeful that I will not fail.

Soon after the six-month mark of Mike's passing, I took a step forward in my life for my son and me, and for Mike. When I was pregnant with Conner, I earned my Master's Degree in Educational Administration. I aspired to be a principal, and Mike was supportive of that professional move. But I never had the opportunity to use the degree while Mike was living.

Early in the school year, a few months before his passing, Mike and I received word that a high school principal position would be available at a neighboring school district. We discussed the opportunity, deciding it was a no-brainer for me to apply when the time came. The position opened a couple of months after Mike's accident; but as Conner and I were not then ready for another huge change, I did not apply.

Months passed, and I received a call that the elementary principal was also leaving this school district. She and I have been friends for years. I talked to Conner and after a long discussion, tears, and prayers, we decided, as a team, that I would apply. He accompanied me when I delivered my application, we spoke with my friend and with the superintendent, then left. I had no expectations. I had no nerves or worries. I was simply dropping off an application.

The following day I received a call to come in for an interview early the next week. Still, I had no expectations. I told myself it was just an interview and no big deal. On the evening of my interview, I looked at myself in the mirror and cried. I was dressed professionally, in a black pencil skirt, black and white polka-dot button up dress shirt, and black heels. My hair was fixed nicely and my face adorned with full makeup for the first time in six months. My mom and sister had come over to help me choose an interview outfit and to stay with Conner while I was gone the next day. I reached down to Mike's Marine Corps ring that adorns my neck. I touched it and told my sister I didn't know if they would like it or not, but I would not take his ring off. I wore it every day and I wanted him with me. She assured me it would be fine.

In that moment I became someone new, someone different from the old me. I looked like a strong, independent, smart, successful woman. Inside I was torn to a million pieces like always; torn between a smile and a tear, a step forward and a crash to my knees. But I had said yes to the interview.

On my drive to the interview, I prayed and asked God to ease my nerves and help me to not sound stupid. I teach interview skills and I did not want to mess that part up!

A few minutes away from my destination, Mike came to me through his song, "Drinking Class." I heard him saying, "You got this, babe. Good job. You're gonna do great."

I parked the truck, climbed down, and took a deep breath as I took my first step forward.

The interview went well and for another week I thought nothing of the job opportunity. I did not lose sleep over it. I did not have butterflies in my stomach. But I did pray. I prayed to God that if it was His will for this change to be good for Conner and me, then it would turn into an offer. If not, then it was a great interview experience anyway. I gave it to God. I trusted Him with whatever came our way, solid in knowing it would be what He wanted for us.

Conner and I went about our regular daily routines for the week following the interview. One evening, we joined some family members for a St. Louis Cardinals' game. After a very long day, I was ready to go to bed in our hotel. I had taken ibuprofen three different times that day due to a headache that would not subside. I was about to roll over and close my eyes when my cell phone rang. I recognized the number as that of the school district where I had applied. It was a job offer to become high school principal.

I asked for ten minutes to discuss it with Conner. In those ten minutes, we cried, prayed, and talked to Daddy. I told Conner that if Mike was still here, we would be having this exact same conversation at this exact same moment because it was what Daddy had wanted me to do. I called the superintendent back with a humble, "yes." Conner and I would begin our new journey in the upcoming school year.

Mike had been gone for six months and four days when I went to the new school to review my contract. I willed myself to ignore the churning in my stomach. I had to ignore the desire to break down and go lie down beside Mike's gravesite and cry for hours. I wanted to spend the entire day beside him, or in bed with the covers over my head.

But I couldn't. I had to breathe. I had to keep stepping. I felt such appreciation and promise at the new opportunity. I was so ready for the appreciation, promise, and excitement to overpower the despair, the confusion, and the feeling of being lost.

The first person I wanted to tell was Mike, to make sure he was proud of me. I wanted to say that I am still moving forward with our plan. I craved his affirmation that I made the right decision by accepting the position. I longed to hear him say, "I'm proud of you, babe." It broke my heart that I couldn't hear his voice of excitement when I told him I got the job. It killed a part of my soul that he could not be part of a celebration of my career, that something we had both worked for could not be shared with my husband.

I miss his voice. I miss talking to him about everything. When life would be "too much," ha . . . if I only knew then what I know now. I used to crave silence. I sometimes needed that quiet, alone time. Not necessarily from anyone or anything specific, but I felt like I needed it. I would sit on the porch alone and Mike would come out to check on me. He asked every time, "What's wrong?" Nothing was wrong; I just needed to escape reality and responsibility for a few minutes and sit with my thoughts.

The silence I live with now is deafening. It is loud with the emptiness I feel. It screams at me that I'm alone on an intimate relationship level. It screams that I am raising a child on my own, often yelling my failures right back at me. The silence screams that I should have done more for Mike, with him. The silence reminds me of what I was so lucky and blessed to have. It yells at me with the ugly reminder of how I lost him, something my brain won't let me forget.

I loved his laugh and his voice; they made me feel sane and safe. I crave them. I crave the stupid noises he would make in his sleep. I crave the loud snoring that kept me awake at night. I crave the loud thud of his steps through our house. I crave every sound he ever made, and I no longer crave the silence. I hate the deafening silence. There are so many things that I love, so many things that I hate, and so many things that I miss each day.

Dear Mike,

Until we meet again . . . I am doing my best. I hope you see that and you know that. I hope you feel the love we have all the way to Heaven.

I miss you more than words, but I can't let that stop me from doing what I was doing before you left. The sadness can't overtake me and my role as a mom and a wife. I am still Conner's mom and I am still your wife. I'm going to make you proud. I can't wait to get to Heaven and tell you all about it.

So, today has been a good day and has put a spark of hope inside my heart. I know I will fall down at different times in my life. I know the sadness of losing you will overtake me again and bring me to my knees, but I'm going to pick myself back up to live a life that will make you proud.

I'm so glad I had thirteen years to be with you. One day the years won't matter, as they won't be counted in numbers. Our time will be limitless.

Chapter Nineteen

REALITY IS RIDICULOUS. I KNOW I HAVE TO LIVE IN IT BUT I don't understand it. One day I am filled with hope, and the next that hope leaves me. It is replaced with grief. Grief needs to be punched in the throat.

After the first two years of widowhood, better days did sometimes arrive. I have laughed more and cried less. There remains the ever-present stress of probate and finances that sometimes makes my chest feel tight and my palms sweat, but for the most part I've been much better.

I did not learn that I would have to open an estate and hire a lawyer until Mike had been gone a few months. I tried to sell one of our pieces of property, only to learn that legally, it was not ours at all. It was his. Only his.

After the first realization of legal issues with property, it seemed to avalanche in front of me. I learned that several pieces of property, not just real estate, but personal property as well, were only in his name. I also learned of a debt load for which I could never have been prepared.

I feel stupid. I feel naïve and ignorant. I feel angry. I feel betrayed in some ways.

Regardless of the legal struggles that still continue, my husband is gone. Nothing else matters. My anger and feelings of betrayal toward my husband are diminished by the sadness that fills me. I cannot stay angry with Mike. I love him and miss him too much to remain angry.

And then someone will say something asinine like, "He did that to protect you," or, "He is in a better place now."

Moments like that trigger the demon inside named Grief.

At the end of those difficult days filled with tears and an ubiquitous ache inside, it seems very strange that Mike is not here beside me. Mike was a part of me and I was a part of him. Now I feel like I'm living without a vital organ, and things don't work the same as before. My brain suffers from widow brain; I forget things if I do not set reminders in my phone. My heart skips beats sometimes, and I have to catch my breath because some memory overwhelms my defenses and I crumble in sobs.

I miss all the little things we would say to each other, telling about our highs and lows of the day. That absence of my favorite confidant is what sometimes sends me into those gut-wrenching sobs that took hold the first few days. I sometimes think, *What did I look like in those moments? What did people think when all of a sudden, in the middle of stories about him, I began the strange pattern of breathing and not breathing, when my sister had to come to my chair and bring me back?*

That wasn't me.

I have never broken down like that except for one other time in my life. I lost my grandpa when I was pregnant with Conner, and I was in a class full of high schoolers when I dropped to my knees and began crying.

Now, unfortunately, it *is* me. Major breakdowns occur on a semi-regular basis in this house. But at least I don't often break down in public.

A part of me is missing. There is no organ donor who can replace the missing piece. There is no fix.

Maybe it wouldn't be so bad if we hadn't been so happy, I don't know. But I'm so sick of the random moments that wash over me for a few crippling minutes.

And during those moments, I become angry. I grow angry for many reasons.

One reason is that my heart and brain cannot fully accept the absence of my husband. I mean, they are supposed to be these super strong organs, so why can't they heal and stop reminding me? Why do they still fill me with shock and surprise that this is my new reality? Why am I surprised when I climb into our bed and Mike is not in his place?

I did not choose for my marriage to end! I did not want this or plan for this, or even prepare myself for this to be a possibility. I have been divorced and it sucked, but at least I was consciously agreeing with my ex-husband that we were divorcing. I didn't ask for the divorce, he did, but at least I followed the steps of signing the papers and agreeing to dissolve five years of marriage.

This time, there was no paper to be signed. No agreeing to let go of the love of my life.

And then, the loneliness. I read recently that loneliness is not a strong enough word to describe widowhood. Amen.

Loneliness sneaks into your world like a vicious snake slithers in the grass, quiet and unnoticed until it strikes. It doesn't matter if I'm in a crowded gym full of lively spectators at a basketball game, or sitting shoulder to shoulder at a Cardinals' game. It doesn't matter if I'm in the middle of preparing questions for upcoming interviews I need to do for my new job, or if I'm surrounded by friends and family at a birthday party.

Loneliness is my constant companion and I hate it. I wish I never knew loneliness existed. And it's like it is bitter and angry with me because it comes when I would rather it stay uninvited.

I also feel like a walking paradox. It sounds crazy to say I am lonely, that loneliness isn't a strong enough word to describe widowhood. And then the next minute, I simply want to be left alone.

Hey Babe,
    I wonder where you are right now. I wonder if you miss me as much as I miss you.

You know, I was proud to be seen with you. You were the most handsome man I had ever known. Your smile stole the room. I miss your eyes and how they sparkled and teased between greens and browns. Your laugh was contagious and made everything fun. I remember how you would throw your head back and clap your hands when something was really funny.

As the years passed, I became proud of you for so many more reasons other than you being the hottest man I'd ever known! Yeah, I learned some your Mike Hollis smooth moves.

Michael, I was so proud to be your wife. You were the hardest working man in my world. I've tasted that level of work these past few months. The other day, as I was spraying electric fence rows with weed killer in the ninety-five-degree sunshine, I cried out of guilt. I beat myself up for not doing that for you. I feel guilty that there were so many more things I obviously could have done for you and with you on the farm or with the concrete business, but when you were here you always told me not to do so much for fear of making me sick or hurting me. You protected me from the difficult work that sometimes became dangerous. I took care of our son, the house, the yard, and you did the farm work. I only helped a little and rode along more often.

I hate that I wasn't there for you more. I feel like if I had been, you would not have had to work so hard and so much.

I was also proud because you were incredibly smart. I remember that when we first began dating, you had only been working for MRWA about a year. You taught for them part of the time; your classes helped so many people become certified to operate water and wastewater plants.

I remember when you would show me some of the math and science formulas for your classes. The first time I was like, "Oh my gosh, you know how to do that?" I did not ask because I doubted your ability or intelligence, although you thought that is what I meant. I asked because I could not do such things. I mean, I'm an English teacher at heart for a reason. I can barely balance a checkbook.

Then you asked, "Did you think I was stupid since I worked for the city? Did you think I just rode around in the truck all day?" Ha! No, that is not what I thought! You were amazing at whatever you did, whether it was farming or teaching, or making me fall in love with you. I just had no idea you were that crazy smart.

I'm still proud to be your wife. I hope you know that. We were supposed to spend the rest of our lives together. We sure were making it, weren't we? We sure were doing great.

I dream of you often. The dreams are so incredibly real it hurts. When I awake, I catch my breath and often times I cry uncontrollably. I can't go back to sleep after those dreams. I hear your voice too. I have your outgoing voicemail message saved on my phone, but I haven't listened in a while. I hear you clearly in my dreams. One dream I had repeatedly for a few nights, months after you left us, was that you came home. My dream played out that we had been through a separation for a few months and you were ready to come home. You realized what you had here and you weren't ready to live without it. I hated that dream.

I fell in love with you quickly. You fell in love with me the same. All those years ago, I feared you would think I was crazy to fall that fast. You were so sweet and affectionate and sincere. I am so glad that you fell for me as hard and as fast as I fell for you.

I found something on Pinterest (someone please help me with my addiction) and it reads: "I was supposed to spend the rest of my life with you and then I realized . . . you spent the rest of your life with me. I smile because I know you loved me till the day you went away. And will keep loving me till the day we're together again." I cannot wait to see you again someday. You better have your feet planted firmly on that Heavenly ground because I am going to come running! I am going to wrap my arms around your neck and kiss you until I can't kiss you anymore. I'm going to smile and cry and yell in delight. I love you more than words baby, now, forever, and always times infinity. I will forever be yours.

Chapter Twenty

When I became a mother a little more than thirteen years ago, I knew I was in for sleepless nights. I prepared myself mentally for the frequent feedings, the diaper changes, the rocking until sleep visited us again briefly, and all that new mom sleep deprivation.

Sleeplessness due to parenting is a whole different ballgame than sleeplessness due to widowhood. In the first year, I awoke around three a.m. every single night.

Sleeplessness still plagues me, hides under my pillow every night, waiting to whisper in my ear, waiting to bring me thoughts I cannot shake.

You're going to be alone forever.

You should be alone forever.

Wait, no you shouldn't.

You should try to meet someone new.

I hope you do meet someone new.

But he will never be like Mike.

You will never find someone like Mike.

Well, maybe you will.

But I doubt it.

You have to think about Conner on every date you might ever go on.

I can't believe you're already thinking about maybe meeting someone new in the future, I don't care how far out you see it.

How dare you consider a new life?

But Mike would want you to.

You guys actually talked about it a long time ago.

You remember, you talked about what you each would do if something happened?

I remember.

You told him to find someone who treated Conner like gold.

You teased him and told him she better not be hot.

He told you to find someone who would be good to Conner and you.

He told you to look for someone who didn't work as hard as he did.

He told you to just try and be happy, it didn't matter who it was with.

He told you he wanted you to be able to be happy again without him, if that ever happened.

Well, it happened, didn't it?

Now what?

What about the bills that are due?

What about your new job?

I know you wish Mike was here for it, but he's not so you might as well get excited and happy about it.

He wants you to be.

It's the job he wanted you to have and you know he's smiling down.

So just be happy about it.

Make a difference.

What if you suck at it?

What if you have all these great ideas and things you want to do and then nobody likes them?

What if Conner hates his new school?

But . . . what if he loves it?

What if you succeed and you become the best principal ever?

When is his tombstone going to be placed?

I know you are ready for it so it kind of honors him and gives you and the boys a place to see him, even if it's not really seeing him.

I wonder if the cows are okay.

You know Mike used to check them all hours of the night.

Maybe you should, too.

But you'll wake Conner.

He would be scared if he woke and you weren't in bed.

So just lie there, the cows are fine.

Okay, shut down.

Go to sleep.

Wait, what do you have on the calendar this week?

And the cycle continues all night, every night.

When I became a new mother and sleep evaded me, I had Mike to lean on and share the sleeplessness with. We would take turns caring for Conner.

I have no one to take turns with now.

I miss having someone.

I miss my husband.

Chapter Twenty-One

I HAVE READ THAT A WIDOWED PERSON'S FIRST BIRTHDAY without his or her spouse is difficult. Difficult does not even touch it. I never expected my birthday to be so sad and lonely. But I cried the entire week leading up to my first birthday without Mike. And I have cried every birthday since.

I've tried pretending. For my first birthday as a widow, I took my son, along with a widow-sister (wister) and her son, on a weekend trip out of town to try and have some birthday fun. I was miserable almost the entire time with spurts of laughter here and there, and then spurts of tears when it was just my friend and me in the room. She understands. Her story is similar to mine.

Her husband was killed in a vehicle accident when her son was very young. She and her husband had been together for thirteen years and married for eleven. Her husband and mine shared similar senses of humor; we both loved our husbands beyond measure.

The hope of distraction on my first birthday and subsequent birthdays does not help.

On my first birthday, when we tried to escape with my wister and her son, we returned home to my family and Mike's family awaiting us. They and my son all had gifts waiting for me. They made lunch and seemed excited to see us. Although I love them with all my heart, at that very moment, I wished nothing more than to be alone. I did not want lunch. I did not want gifts. I did not want to talk. I did not want to eat or laugh or anything.

I wanted to sleep. I wanted to lay beside my husband's grave. I wanted to run away.

But I did not want to hurt anyone's feelings. They miss him too, and they want to help me smile again. So, I partook of lunch and cake and then it was time for gifts. I had been gritting my teeth so hard my jaws hurt. I was trying my best to look happy. I know it was an epic fail but at least I tried.

And then my little boy gave me a beautiful watch as a gift and I lost it. Mike had given me a beautiful watch as a gift years ago. I began crying and then sobbing and then I cried out, "He should be here."

I closed my eyes through the pain but could hear my poor momma's sobs and my mother-in-law's apologies as she held on to my shoulders. My son came to a chair right next to the recliner, the exact same way he did the day his daddy died. And *that* is what brought me out of it enough that I could finally breathe. I could not be that woman again. I could not let my little boy go back in time, although I know we both do it every day. He misses his daddy just like I do. And I can't fix it.

I told everyone I felt tired. After I could breathe steadily, everyone gathered their things, hugged me and told me they loved me, and left. I hugged my son and told him how sorry I was for breaking down.

He grabbed me by the arms and said, "Mom . . . never say you're sorry for crying about Dad. It's okay. Everybody knows. But never say you're sorry."

Wow. That's my son. That's my husband right there in the grown up man voice Conner sometimes uses, even at the age of eleven. I am beyond proud of my little man.

I was so drained that I went to rest on the couch and slept for two hours.

I dreamed of him while I slept. I could taste the salt on his lips when he came in and kissed me after working all day. I felt the rough callouses on his hands as he laced his fingers with mine. I smelled on him what lots of women might complain about, the smell of dirt and hard work. I felt his whiskers as he snuggled next to me and kissed the back of my neck. I saw the mischief in his eyes when he smiled at me.

I felt him. I heard him.

And then I awoke.

My sister told me that surely my first birthday without Mike would be manageable because I made it through Mike's birthday, Mother's Day, Father's Day, Fourth of July, Conner's birthday, and so on. She was wrong. My first birthday alone was just as difficult as all the other holidays. Every "first" will be difficult. Probably every "seventh" or "tenth" will too. I turned thirty-seven. Alone. I have since turned thirty-eight and thirty-nine alone. My life *was* where it was supposed to be seven short months before that first birthday without him. Life was everything I had dreamed of and planned for. My husband was the man of my dreams, and he loved me.

I assume all my birthdays, and all holidays, will remain difficult. Why? Because I haven't stopped loving him. I didn't get the choice to say it was over. I didn't fall out of love and move on. He is my husband. Still. Always.

The week of my first birthday without Mike continued in ridiculous fashion. Following a week full of crying that led up to my birthday, not much improved. In fact, it went from bad to worse.

Mid-week, I helped my mom babysit my niece, Reagan, while my sister took my other niece, Alyssa, to the dentist. I was thinking about how this marked seven months without Mike, but decided to make the most of my time with Reagan.

However, my son had different plans.

I heard a blood-curdling scream from outside and rushed to the door. Conner attempted to park our Ranger on the back concrete patio; there is ample room between two large posts and he parks it there often. That day, he paid too much attention to what was playing on the living room TV, which he could see through the sliding glass door, and not enough attention on where he steered the Ranger.

Conner rammed the edge of the Ranger, along with his left arm, into one of the large posts of the concrete patio. Through screams and tears, he explained that his arm hurt very badly. I remained calm and convinced him to rest on the couch long enough for me to inspect the injury.

Conner wailed through the pain. He continued to hold his left arm just above his wrist. Tears ran down his face. He was sweaty and breathing rapidly as panic set it. I helped focus his breathing so I could inspect his arm. On the inside I was a hot mess.

Once Conner's breathing settled, we rushed to our local clinic for X-rays to confirm that his arm was broken. I kept my composure but longed to have Mike with us. He should have been there! Conner wanted his dad. He needed his dad. And I was angry and broken all at once.

The night was restless for us both. Conner tried to sleep but whimpered and whined in his sleep because of the pain.

My first birthday without my husband sucked. That entire week sucked. And I had to do it all alone. Just like every other day of my life since Mike left this world.

Dear Michael,

You come to me in my dreams.

Sometimes I dream we are in a huge fight, yelling and screaming, and breaking up. I guess that's my mind's way of trying to force myself to accept that you're gone.

Other times, my dreams are like our life used to be, such as last night's dream.

We had arranged for Conner to have a sitter. The house was lit with candles and I had dressed specially for you in a black dress and black heels. My hair was down and curled, like you loved it. My makeup was applied perfectly with the perfect tint of pink lipstick.

Dinner was cooked and in the oven staying warm, and a bottle of wine was chilled and ready to pour. When you walked into the house, exhausted from your day's work, you smiled as you saw me round the corner. I had soft music playing in the background and I came to you and kissed you hello.

Right there in our kitchen we slow danced. You were wearing your beat up boots and dirty clothes. Your left arm was wrapped around my waist, and your right hand held my left.

I let my fingers gently lace through yours and let my right hand rest on your shoulder. You smiled and talked low, telling me what a nice surprise it was to come home to a woman who loved you and wanted to make you happy.

It felt so good to have you in my arms and for me to be wrapped in yours. I woke up crying, hating myself for dreaming this dream. It hurts so badly to dream of how life used to be and I can't imagine ever slow dancing with anyone else in our kitchen.

Time is not making things any easier or less painful. Luckily, work is a great distraction, but when I'm not there, my mind travels to you every second. It seems that everywhere I go, and no matter who is with me, I become misty-eyed because I look around and feel so alone.

I wonder how long I will feel this way. I wonder how long my life will seem incomplete. You were my world . . . my safe place . . . my best friend and confidant . . . my fighting partner who was worth fighting for . . . my soul mate.

I miss your hands around me; I miss our slow dances in the kitchen; I miss our love and marriage and friendship and plans of forever. Thanksgiving and Christmas are just around the corner and I suppose my heart is missing you even more.

I watched a Hallmark movie last night about a widow at Christmas. I related to the character; at one point she said, "I'm trying to not hate Christmas."

I'm trying too. I'm trying to not hate Thanksgiving, Christmas, Mondays in general, the 29th of every month, and so on. I'm trying to not hate being a single mom, or myself. I'm trying to not hate all of the debt I was left with, and all of the responsibilities that came with this huge debt load. I'm trying to not hate the man I've never even met, who answered my husband's phone that day and told me he had passed away. I really am trying.

I spoke with my mom earlier today and she told me something that makes it even harder to not hate myself as a widow.

She told me that my son was sitting at the table the other day, a day when I was at a principal conference in a different town and he stayed the day with Grandma. He sat at the table and was making a rubber band ball. Mom was watching TV and Conner said, "Grandma, I miss Dad. When Dad was here, he would have been sitting right here beside me with his laptop and would have looked over here and said, 'I love you, son, and you have an incredible imagination.' I sure wish he was here. And if Mom was okay, Grandma, I will be okay. God helps me be okay, but I need Mom to be okay, and then I can be, too."

Wow. I have obviously failed to epic proportions since my husband passed away. I have cried so much. I have withdrawn myself from so many people and places and things from our past life. It is a past life, one that is not ours anymore. Conner and I have a new life, whether it is one for which we planned or not. Whether it is one for which we are prepared or not, it is ours. Just him and I.

I have spent so many days still dressed in my pajamas, taking a nap when I could, watching TV in silence, staying in the recliner while my little boy played on the floor alone. While he watched TV in the other room. While he went to our bedroom and played X-Box.

My depression, my sadness, my loneliness has to step aside so I can go back to being a mom. That was my dream all along . . . to be a mom. You may have left me to finish the job alone, but God has never left me. I have turned my cheek to Him, and tried to ignore the tug on my heart to return to a church these last few months. I have tried to pretend my faith is still strong and that I am still a good mom.

But all of the pretending is doing me no good. So today I have to change things. I have to set my mind straight. I cannot fail. I cannot let my little boy grow up thinking his mom will never be okay again; worrying that Mommy will be sad forever and we will never be genuinely happy again. I love you with all of my heart; I miss you with every fiber of my being. But it's time I let your memory live inside my heart as a driving force to do better, not to give up and sit idly by as my son grows up without the mom I was born to be.

I love you, baby, and I'm going to keep my promise to you the day you left me and I held your hand closely. I promised you on that day, and the day we lowered you into the cold December ground, that I would do my best to raise our boy alone.

NFAxI, your wife

Chapter Twenty-Two

GRIEF IS A CONSTANT WAVE. ONE DAY WE LAUGH AND smile and try our best to heal our broken hearts, and the next we try to force the breaths to come easily instead of in broken sobs.

I found a chart on Pinterest once, demonstrating the stages of grief. A cute little bell curve with stages like denial, acceptance, hope, blah, blah, blah. The bell curve just moves along in this beautiful pattern of a perfect progression.

Well, it's a bunch of crap.

It looks so simple. Like learning to live without my husband should be this nice easy flow, and once I hit rock bottom of guilt, loneliness, and isolation, I can only go up!

Lies.

Nothing about me losing my husband, and the boys losing their dad, flows in an easy pattern. No one's grief does. That is the most idiotic concept ever.

One day in particular that brought a tidal wave of grief, one that was off that stupid chart, was the first time Conner saw his dad's headstone. Months after Mike passed, the stone was finally placed.

No one can prepare grievers for choosing a stone. It is a long process to not only choose a proper stone, but then also to have the company place the stone. Then viewing the placed stone for the first time is another tedious process. Courage has to be built up before someone grieving feels ready to view the stone.

Conner hadn't seen his dad's stone yet; he had wanted no part of choosing it. I didn't either; but it was my job to choose the perfect stone to honor my husband, not only for me and the boys, but for Mike's family, too. I chose a light, maroon-colored stone. I did not want gray or black. The stone is slanted, similar to Mike's dad's stone, located right beside Mike's. The process of choosing Mike's stone was done entirely via email. I could not force myself to physically visit the monument company and look through stones, like I was buying a new car.

Etched into the stone is a farm scene: cows, bales of hay, and a fence, along with Mike's name, the two dates, and *We Love You Forever.*

I was nervous about taking Conner to see it. I knew he would feel like I had—indescribable shock and pain. We arrived at the cemetery and Conner and I walked over together. Usually on our visits, we take turns talking to Mike alone. We will sit together at his grave, but also give each other time alone to say what is in our hearts. Sometimes we say nothing at all.

As we stepped together to Mike's tombstone, Conner straightened the flags and flowers that Mike had been given, and then he sat on a camouflage blanket I brought. Conner's hand rubbed over the words. Over the cow and hay bale. Over his dad's name. He bowed his head and rested upon his knees in front of his dad.

Through my own tears, I told my son I loved him, and took my place under a big shady tree to await my turn. I sat in silence beneath the shade tree, lost in my own thoughts. When Conner walked back to me, I lost control of my emotions. I hugged him close, sobbing and telling him how sorry I am that we have to come to a cemetery to see his dad. It shouldn't be this way.

But our resilient boy, whose heart is made of pure gold, looked up at me, removed his hat, kissed me, and said, "It's gonna be okay, Mom. I love you."

After I finally released Conner from our embrace, it was my turn. Watching our son talk to the stone for the first time broke my heart. I fell to the blanket on my knees, feeling helpless, hopeless, in shock and disbelief, and completely broken.

I reached out to touch my husband's name. Crying, I told him how much I love and miss him. I cried out about how unfair it is that Conner and I have to come here to be with him.

So, that ridiculous-looking chart of the "stages of grief" I found on Pinterest is crap. There is *no* smooth sailing through this process. I sometimes wonder if it goes on and on forever. Probably.

It's not simple.

It's not easy.

We do not go through this emotion, then move to that emotion, then on to the next in some perfect healing order. We fall after we have climbed partway up the mountain. We topple over in the blink of an eye after we have risen to new heights. Grief is an up and down battle that we will fight for the rest of our lives.

Or so I've been told. This I believe. Not some chart on Pinterest.

I imagine that years will pass, and some days I will still have a hard time breathing. I imagine I'll be doing fine when suddenly something will trigger a memory, and I'll come crashing down.

Grief is a monster. It robs us of our happiness, our hopes, and our will to move forward. It sneaks in when least expected and stays well past its welcome. And then when we have become accustomed to its presence and it leaves momentarily, we almost come to crave it. Like it has become our best friend, without whom we cannot imagine living.

We imagine true happiness becoming ours again someday. Does fear still exist? Sadness, loneliness, insecurities? You bet. But we adjust. We adjust our sails to traverse the waters of our newfound selves, our widow selves. We learn to live with the grief, to live in the grief.

Grief exhausts me. On one hand, I'm sick of it. Grief is a coward, slipping in for sneak attacks when our backs are turned. When we least expect a visit, grief is like the unwanted visit from the Bubonic Plague.

On the other hand, while it may seem insane to say, I am scared to let grief go. I am scared to lock the door and keep grief out, for fear it will build momentum and worsen. I am afraid it will sprout alien tentacles and begin to form inside me until it rips me open from the inside. So, I open the door and, against my own will, I let grief in. I allow it to overtake my personal space. I allow the visits to overtake my heart. I am too weak to turn grief away. And every single "first" without Mike weakens me further.

For example, the first fall season without Mike was the most ridiculous stretch of four months. Fall hunting seasons, Halloween, Thanksgiving, Christmas, and then the one-year mark all follow each other in torturous fashion. The succession of these events dims my mood and creates apprehension about each one.

In our area of the country, and especially in this area of Missouri, gigging season is a time-honored tradition. Gigging is a hunting sport that takes place on the river, with boats and long wooden or fiberglass poles fashioned with large metal, three-pronged forks on the end.

A person stands on the front deck of a boat and attempts to stab a fish with the forked gig pole, while the boat is being motored by another person. The water's current creates difficulty with spotting the fish on the river bed; and all the elements together create a challenge in gigging the fish. Once a "mess" of fish, enough to meet regulations, is acquired, a fish fry dinner takes place.

Mike loved gigging season. He loved the competitive nature he and I shared when gigging. He loved the fish fries on the river bank with potatoes, breaded and fried fish, hush puppies, and of course, cold Bud Light. Mike's favorite part of gigging season was always the laughs shared with family and friends.

With deer season, camps are set up all over the county. Our farm becomes a hub of activity with preparing hunting gear, sighting in rifles to ensure accuracy, gathering snacks for the hunt, and preparing a home-cooked meal for all the hunters. Harvesting meat each year provides our family with a freezer full of prepared venison meals. Mike was always a good shot and enjoyed hunting with his sons and me.

One thing that has made both gigging and deer seasons difficult is that I feel like Conner and I will be a burden to others. Feeling burdensome is another widow reality.

We always had Mike to take us hunting or gigging. We had Mike to get everything ready from making sure the generator was full of gas, that the gigging lights were bright enough and on right, to organizing all our supplies, to purchasing hunting and fishing licenses and tags well in advance. Mike always made gigging and hunting fun.

Now, we usually call someone to take us. We call our friends to ask if they have room in their boat for two more. We call someone, usually my dad, if we harvest a deer. We are forced to rely on someone else.

I write to Mike and talk to him often. Sometimes I just have to talk to him, to pour myself out into words to him. Because too often the grief takes over, and I cannot speak at all.

> Michael,
> I cannot believe that eight months have passed since I last heard your voice in person—rather than in an old home video or the outgoing message from your cell phone, which I saved on my phone.
> I cannot believe it has been eight whole months since I wrapped my arms around you while we stood in the kitchen. Or since you turned to face me and wrapped your arms around me while I buried my face in your chest.
> I cannot believe it has been eight whole months since you kissed me goodbye and told me you loved me before you opened the sliding glass door to leave for work. Or since we talked about the plans for our day, and what might be good for dinner.
> I cannot believe I no longer have your dirty laundry in the hamper, or your coffee cup in the sink. I cannot adjust

to sleeping on your side of the bed while Conner sleeps on mine.

I cannot understand how when we take rides through the farm on the Ranger, you are not down at the machine shed working on a piece of equipment. I cannot fathom the absence of your smell on my skin or the salty taste of your kiss when you return home from work in the evenings.

I cannot believe that I no longer see you smiling after you are showered and dressed for a date night. You would wear your "sexy jeans" that I bought for you from Gap after our first year together. You saved those jeans for our dates and for work conferences, but only if I was there.

I cannot believe I no longer have your hand to hold while we walk around Wal-Mart looking in the sporting goods section for the millionth time, not buying anything.

I cannot understand how I must take our little boy to a tombstone to talk to his dad when he is so young.

There are so many things I cannot believe . . . that I cannot wrap my mind around . . . that I cannot prepare myself to accept or understand.

I haven't the energy to write much tonight, as my soul has been drained these last few days. I have cried almost every day this week while I drove home from work. Once, it came so powerfully I could barely see to drive.

I miss you more than anyone could possibly understand. God bless them . . . it's not their fault they don't have the right words. No one does.

I hope Heaven is amazing and that you are exactly like I imagine . . . young, happy, smiling, warm, chatting with your dad, tipping your head back in laughter while you clap your hands together, energetic, rested, carefree, unscathed, perfect.

I love you.

NFAxI, your wife

Chapter Twenty-Three

ONCE WE SURVIVED OUR FIRST OF THE FALL HUNTING seasons without Mike, we decided to boycott Thanksgiving. I knew we could not boycott Christmas, so we took our small victory where we could. We spent part of Thanksgiving Day watching a movie in an almost empty theater.

As our first Christmas without Mike approached, I knew that no one in our family would allow us to skip Christmas like we had Thanksgiving. I dreaded Christmas. I cried pretty much every day from Thanksgiving on, knowing that Christmas Day would punch me in the gut.

One night I felt Mike's presence on my heart and knew there were words he wanted our boy to hear.

Hey Bubba,
Merry Christmas! I'm so sorry I can't be there with you today. I know it's hard and I know it hurts, but you have so many people surrounding you who love you, son.

I watched you open your presents last night at Grandma Jackie's. That *Furious 7* car looks pretty cool! I could see how fast it went all the way from up here! I saw how big you're getting too, and how grown up.

I can't believe how much you've grown in a year. It's crazy! I saw how grown up you were when your mom cried last night too, son. I'm sorry about that. I know Momma is trying hard to keep everything together, but she couldn't quit thinking about all the Christmases we had, and it was too much for her.

I know sometimes you worry she'll never be happy again. But she will. In time. You just need to be patient with her, Con. Okay? She's got more on her plate than any woman should have, and I get mad at myself for leaving it all on her shoulders.

I loved your mom so much when I was there. I would do anything to take away her pain, to make things easier with money, and the lawyers, and all that junk. If I can tell you anything about all this mess, Bub, it's to learn from Daddy's mistakes. No matter what you want out of life, make darn sure your family will be taken care of if anything happens to you. You understand?

But hey, enough of all that sad stuff. Let me tell you about Christmas in Heaven!

It is the most beautiful thing I've ever seen, well, besides you and your brother. The angels sing all the time, and it is music like I've never heard. There is a huge tree in the middle of a golden street and it's all lit up with lights as bright as the stars! There are no presents, of course, but there is sunshine and warmth and all the happy memories of our favorite Christmases on Earth. The smell of homemade sugar cookies fill the air, delicious food is spread all across a huge table, and everyone visits while we watch our families below celebrate Jesus. He is so proud on this day. He sits back with us, just as normal as you or me, and watches us and you all with the biggest and brightest smile I've ever seen.

I can't even describe how much peace there is up here, Son. I smile all the time! I'm warm and covered in sunshine all day long. I'm so young and handsome, if I do say so myself. I feel so good it's crazy!

One day you'll know how it feels up here. One day, a long time from now in your time, but it'll seem like a minute to me, you'll come and see Heaven too. You'll hear the angels singing, and feel the sunshine wash all over you. You'll skip around like a little boy. I think that's how I'll get to see you when you come. I think you'll be my little boy when you come and we won't ever even know we were apart. It'll be just like I went to work for a bit and came back home.

But for now, you have to live. Live a life full of love, Conner. Don't hold anger inside, don't hold sadness over losing me. Cover it with so much fun that it hides away in the back and doesn't control your life.

Keep doing well in school and get that math grade up, boy. Try hard, okay? Ask for help. Not just with math either, but with life. Don't be too proud not to ask for help, like me. I should have asked more. But grow and learn and laugh and love and make memories that will keep you smiling for years to come.

Hug your momma tight for me, son. Tell her I love her and miss her with all my might. And the same goes for you and your brother. You three were the best things to ever happen to me. I wish I had shown that more often by not working as much, but I can't take it back now. Just know I never once didn't love you more than anything in this world.

So, Merry Christmas, my boy. Have fun opening presents and remember I'm still right there with you, buddy, in the stories you guys tell of me, in the candles you burn for me, and more importantly, in your heart forever. I love you.

Daddy

That first Christmas without Mike was just as awful as I anticipated it would be. I cried through it all. Pain surged through my stomach. The shaking returned, and I could not force myself to eat more than a few bites. I produced the obligatory smile with each gift my family opened. I felt alone and empty, though we were surrounded by family. My happy family's tradition of Christmas celebration was gone. And in its place came pain and sorrow, regret and loneliness, anger, and fear.

Our tradition always unfolded in the same fashion: Christmas Eve morning and evening were spent with my family, Christmas morning was with the boys, and Christmas afternoon with Mike's family.

We used to have breakfast at my dad's, then join my mom in the evening for dinner and gifts. For Christmas Eve breakfast, my stepmom Margaret prepared a huge spread: biscuits and gravy, bacon and sausage, fried eggs, and juice. The smells permeated to the front yard, and we smelled the teasing scents as soon as we exited our vehicles. The small trailer where my dad and stepmom live made for a warm welcome from the cold December weather. If snow was on the ground, we would go outside for a snowball fight. We would share gifts, coffee, good food, and laughter.

We used to celebrate Christmas Eve with my mom and my sister and her family. My sister and I took turns hosting each year and I always loved when it was my turn. I have enjoyed cooking my whole life; I learned by watching my mom and my grandpa. My excitement would grow for the day's meal as soon as I purchased the groceries weeks in advance.

The day usually began with prepping the turkey or ham, organizing all the sides on the kitchen counter, and laying out decorations, plates, and glasses. I would cook in the early morning hours while Mike worked on the farm. Conner often played in the floor with his new toys from our visit to my dad's that morning while I cooked and listened to Christmas music in the background. With childlike excitement, I prepped food, cleaned the house, lit candles, and eagerly awaited my family's arrival.

On Christmas morning, we always shared gifts with each other and with both boys. Mike and I would sit beside each other on one side of the living room, and the boys would sit beside each other on the other side. A hot cup of coffee in hand, I would snuggle next to my husband as the boys opened gifts. Mike would place his hand on my back or on my shoulders and play with my hair while he smiled at the joy on everyone's faces.

After opening gifts, we'd relax and watch the boys play with their new gifts. Mike would feed the cows and I would ride with him. After that he'd rest, watch TV, watch the boys play, and snuggle with me on the couch. That evening we would go to his mom's for our final Christmas dinner and then sit together on the couch while we watched TV again.

I miss his hand on my back, playing with my hair. I miss him sitting beside me, occasionally stealing a kiss. I miss his warmth, his tenderness. I miss how relaxed he was, not worrying about work. I miss his laugh and his smile as he would ask the boys to show him their gifts. He would say, "Oh, cool! What's that? Let me see!" It didn't matter that he already knew what the gifts were, he still acted surprised and impressed with each one.

My first Christmas as a widow, I sat alone on the couch. I watched alone while my son opened his gifts. I did not feel my husband's hand on my back; I did not hear his laugh or see his shining smile. I did not get to snuggle beside him on the couch, or ride around checking and feeding the cows, sitting close beside him in the truck. I did not get dressed up to try and look good for him. I did not get lost in his eyes like I did every day for thirteen years.

I did it alone. Surrounded by family, I was alone. I sat in silence while I tried to muster the strength to smile for our son. I felt only the cold empty space next to me, and within me, instead of the warmth of my husband's love. I faked every smile and every laugh. I held back the tears as long as I could for our son's sake. And it all made me sick to my stomach.

The first Christmas without Mike was abysmal. The others to follow have been just as terrible. I don't know how time will make his absence any less painful. I don't know how my life will ever seem real without Mike. I am trying my best to put one foot in front of the other and to keep my mind focused on making a better and easier life for my son and me, but some days wear me out.

The wrinkles in the corners of his eyes.

The way his smile filled a room.

His chuckle that was so cute and contagious, which I teased him about.

His hands.

Scarred from years of hard work.

Gentle when he held me.

Patient when he was showing our little boy how to do something for the first time.

The way one eye was greener than the other.

His dimples that were usually hidden by facial hair.

His random decision to shave his beard into a Fu Manchu, even though I hated it.

The way he wanted to look nice for me on date night.

Date nights.

At home, or out and about . . . it didn't matter to me.

The way he would dress in a suit and go to prom with me, even though he hated it.

Slow dances in the kitchen.

Sneaking up on him to listen while he was singing to our baby boy.

The raspy tone in his voice.

The way he told me I was beautiful every single day.

The way that he meant it.

How tough he was.

His strength, both physically and mentally.

The way he cried when no one but me was looking.

Knowing why he cried and being the only one who knew.

His dark skin tanned by the hours he worked in the sun year-round.

His work ethic.

His desire to build a life for his boys.

His love of farming.

His sometimes not-so-friendly, passionate vernacular when dealing with cows.

His stories—of his Marine Corps days, of his Grandma Holly and Grandma Mary, of his dad.

His skills, being able to do anything he set his mind to.

He never failed.

His determination to succeed.

His ability to learn something new and be almost an expert by the second time he did it.

His math skills.

His romantic side.

The way he would come up behind me and put his arms around my waist and his chin on my shoulder.

The way he would look at me, and really look at me, loving every part of me.

When he would kiss me on the back of the neck.

When he would hold me, just stand there and hold me close to him and tell me over and over how lucky he was to have me.

He loved me at my worst.

He liked my old, torn, holey farm jeans and baseball cap.

He wanted me.

He made me feel safe and secure.

He dreamed of a future with me.

When we would lie down and start talking and end up laughing until we had to make each other shut up and go to sleep.

The way he had special nights in the living room floor on a pallet with his sons.

His surprises.

His selflessness when it came to helping others.

His silly side.

The "wiggle" in his walk.

His lips.

His kisses.

Holding his hand.

His compliments about the house on a day when I had cleaned for two hours.

His appreciation of a good meal.

His pride when he was with his family.

The one phrase he would yell at every basketball game: "Shoot the ball!"

The way he would sit with Conner and the laptop to look at cars, guns, toys, or whatever else Conner wanted to look at.

Every little thing.

That is what I miss.

It is difficult to find joy in things now. I miss everything about him, about us, about happiness, and about life.

Mike brought me joy. He brought joy to everything we did together. Please don't think I'm being terrible and neglectful and unappreciative of what I still have. I love and cherish every person in my life and every blessing sent from God. One day, hopefully, the joy will return to my heart.

Can you imagine what it would be like without your number one partner? Can you take the time to stop, turn and look at him, and imagine everything you love about him suddenly vanishing? Can you fathom the idea of never seeing your one true love again? Never hearing the voice that calms you in the night? Never kissing those lips that melt you? Never holding the hand which brings you comfort?

I never imagined those things and yet here I am, living them. And it is torture.

Conner feels it, too. Conner continued struggling at our new school. The support we received from the school counselor, nurse, my secretary, and others was immeasurable. But it has been in vain. Conner just cannot grasp life without his dad.

I remember one particular day when school was hectic; Conner cried a few times, and I was completely worn out. Conner had visited the counselor's office multiple times that morning, until she finally allowed him to work in her office the remainder of the day. I felt defeated. I began to second-guess my decision to take the position as principal and move schools. But God and Mike sent me what I needed.

One of my teachers told me he knew God put me in the position of his high school principal, a job for which he himself applied. He told me I was doing a great job, and I needed the principal job in order to focus on something other than losing Mike.

Another teacher told me she adored me and was so happy to come to work every day, because of the way I ran our school and supported my staff and students. A fellow administrator volunteered to supervise a ballgame so I could have an evening off. A teacher stopped by after our staff meeting to see how things were going.

And in time, God brought us back to our home school, back to what Conner needed: family and friends. God put people and circumstances we needed in our paths on many occasions to help me make it through the tough days.

Chapter Twenty-Four

For our second Christmas without Mike, I surprised Conner with concert tickets and a weekend trip to Chicago. We have always been a musical family. Conner and I find refuge in music. Fortunately, I found tickets to a concert tour of Lee Brice and Justin Moore. Finding the two on tour together was serendipitous. Justin Moore is one of Conner's favorite artists, and Lee Brice's song "The Drinking Class" was Mike's favorite song.

I surprised Conner with the tickets on Christmas morning. We could not wait for our January weekend in Chicago. Although apprehensive, I was a woman on a mission. We would go to Chicago and have a wonderful time.

The weekend finally arrived and we set off. I carried my pocket knife in my purse. We stood in awe at the size of our hotel: The Crowne Plaza in Rosemont, Illinois. It doesn't take much to impress us country folk, but this was a very nice hotel.

After unpacking in our room, we ventured to the hotel restaurant and ate the best spaghetti and meatballs ever.

Our first night we recovered from eating way too much of our delicious dinner, while planning our trip into the city the following day. Morning arrived, and we hailed a taxi, pocket knife still in my purse.

We visited Shedd Aquarium, The Bean, Navy Pier, and Willis Tower, where we walked out onto the sky deck and survived! Everyone we encountered was nice to us. Not one person proved rude or shady. Well, one guy did, but we just crossed the street to walk away from him.

At the Shedd Aquarium, I noticed a security guard checking bags. I figured I better have a conversation with the security guard about my pocket knife. I explained that I am a country girl who lives on a farm, and has never visited Chicago. My pocket knife offers me some small sense of safety.

He said, "Well, follow me." He pointed to a yellow caution cone by an empty foyer and said, "I can't hide your knife or hold it for you. But you can slide it under this cone. When you come back out, just make eye contact with me and I'll let you go get it."

After Shedd Aquarium, we toured Navy Pier. We had a fun little selfie photoshoot on the ferris wheel, ate yummy Chicago snacks, and watched the boats in the pier. The sun shone on us through the cold winter day, and our hearts were warm with so many blessings.

After spending a beautiful day sightseeing, evening approached for the concert. Our blessings had just begun.

After we got all gussied up, Conner and I walked across the street to the Rosemont Theater. As we entered, we noticed two things: a table of artist apparel and a Justin Moore guitar. Immediately Conner's eyes shot straight at the guitar. On top of the guitar rested a note that read, "Buy Me and get Meet and Greet passes!"

Conner was elated when I purchased the guitar, and we were both excited for the Meet and Greet. I had never before purchased Meet and Greet passes at a concert. Seeing our excitement, a young lady asked if we'd like a photo taken in front of the radio station backdrop.

We had our photo taken with the sweetest young ladies from Chicago 95.5, and Conner had his taken with his new guitar. One of the young ladies, Brooke, hugged me and asked, "So, what brings you guys to Chicago to the show tonight?"

"Well, actually, this is a very special concert for us," I replied. "My husband passed away almost two years ago. Conner loves music, and Justin Moore's music has helped him to heal some. Many of his lyrics remind him of his dad."

Brooke listened intently as I continued.

"And Lee Brice's song 'The Drinking Class' was one of Mike's favorite songs. So, when I found them together, it just had to happen."

Brooke's eyes filled with tears. "Wow. Where are you guys from?"

I explained that we had driven seven hours one way from Missouri, and that we had just experienced a magical day in Chicago.

"What seats do you guys have? Are they good?" asked Brooke.

I opened the ticket app on my phone and showed her.

"Oh, those are pretty good seats," Brook said, "but you know what would be even better?"

I did not know. A million dollars? Lee Brice to be single?

"Pit passes!"

And she got us free pit passes for the concert! Conner and I stood in disbelief and awe.

Our blessings multiplied as the evening passed. During our Meet and Greet with Justin Moore, we received an autograph for the guitar and posed for a photo with Justin.

He asked Conner, "Hey man, what is this, date night?"

Conner just grinned and Justin said, "That's all right, buddy. My mom's my best friend, too."

Once the concert began, Conner and I could not fathom how blessed we had been already in our short time in Chicago. On top of all the pleasantries from every person we met during our sightseeing in the city, everyone at the concert was so nice and complimentary.

At one point, a man in a white T-shirt tapped me on the shoulder and said, "Hey, it is so awesome watching you and your son interact here! You guys look like you're having a great time!"

We had to shout to hear each other. "Thanks! We are!"

Throughout the evening, other people tapped me on the shoulder to say how much they enjoyed seeing Conner and me having such a great time. It was crazy how many people commented to us.

Throughout Justin Moore's set on stage, he focused attention on my son. At one point, Justin reached across the group in front of us and handed Conner a guitar pick! He continually fist bumped, high fived, or winked at Conner. My cheeks hurt from smiling so much!

Toward the end of Justin's set, he reached over the group one last time to hand Conner a drum stick!

By the time Lee Brice took the stage, Conner and I just stood in awe. Neither one of us could believe that Justin Moore had been so gracious during his set, or that so many strangers had commented to me! Throughout our conversations with these strangers, I had explained how special we felt being at the concert. I explained the significance of Justin Moore's music for Conner's healing, and Lee Brice's song for a connection to Mike.

I spoke many silent prayers that evening, praising God for bringing us to Chicago safely and for bringing us so many angels.

After Lee Brice soon took the stage and began his set, Conner's anxiety took over. He looked at me with tears in his eyes and said, "Mom, I don't think I wanna be in here when he sings Dad's song."

Oh, my baby boy. My heart grew heavy. I left for the venue foyer with Conner. We immediately spotted Brooke, the young lady who had given us the pit passes.

"Hey, guys! How's it goin' in there?" she asked.

"Well, Conner is kinda feeling anxious about seeing Lee Brice perform his dad's song, so we stepped out for a little bit of a break."

Brooke tilted her head to the side and smiled, "Oh, man, I get it. You wanna stay out here with me so your mom can see it?"

Conner agreed to stay in the foyer with Brooke, at least until I could hear Mike's song. Then I said we would leave after "Drinking Class."

When Mike's song began, emotions overwhelmed me. Every word of the lyrics touched my heart and reminded me once more of how amazing my husband was. Of how amazing our little boy is. Of how amazing our God is for filling our lives with the experience of our Chicago weekend. I recorded Lee Brice singing so that I could hold that memory forever.

Just before exiting the pit to return to Conner, a young lady tapped me on the shoulder. I turned to her as she took my hand in hers.

She said, "Everyone in this pit has watched you and your son all night long. It has been so incredible watching you two have fun and laugh and smile and hug. I swear we've enjoyed watching you guys as much if not more than the concert!"

I smiled and thanked her. But she wasn't finished yet.

"There was a guy here in a white T-shirt earlier and he asked that I give you something." She handed me three hundred dollars. "He asked me to give you this money. It's to help pay for your hotel since you guys had to drive so far to get here, and since it has been such a special concert to you guys."

I looked for the man in the white T-shirt and spotted him running up the aisle to the exit. I guess he did not want recognition for his kind gesture, but just wanted to help us. He wanted to help us enjoy our weekend. He blessed us more than he could ever know. I thanked her, and we exchanged hugs.

When we returned to our hotel, Conner and I shared tears. We talked about Mike for a long time, something we had not done for quite some time. We just sat and talked. My son is such an amazing young man. He is resilient in the midst of tragedy and heartbreak. He builds in me a desire to move forward, a desire to live again. Every single day. I wish his dad could see it all too.

Mike is missing his little boy growing up. He has missed birthdays and holidays, successes and failures. Mike has missed laughter and tears, sicknesses and happy days.

Mike won't get to see Conner dressed up for his first prom. He won't get to watch him graduate and walk across the stage to receive his diploma. Mike will miss watching our boy fall in love for the first time, and he'll miss the day our son marries his true love.

Mike will not be here to meet his grandchildren. There are so many things he will miss, and it breaks my heart every day.

And our boy misses his dad.

Conner came home from school one day several months after Mike passed, and told me that he had his first girlfriend. They, of course, did not actually date or anything, but they talked at school and texted some in the evenings. Being the helicopter mom that I am, I checked all messages. He grew pretty tired of me reading his messages over his shoulder.

After only a couple of days of this first relationship, he almost broke up with her, just because his dad wasn't here to talk him through it. I cried with him the morning he woke at four a.m., doubting himself because Mike wasn't there to tell him what to say.

I told Conner I could handle this. I know what's good to say to girls and what isn't . . . but it's not the same. Boys need their dads.

There will be those special times when our boy would rather have his dad here. And it will be for the simple things, such as taking him bow hunting or riding around on the farm. It will also be for those huge moments in life that take your breath away. And there will be a void as big as the sky.

As a mom, it is difficult to see your child unhappy. He cries often. He talks about his dad and wants to hear stories about us. When Conner pulls on his cowboy boots, I see Michael. Mike pulled on his boots every day in that same exact chair.

Slow dancing with our boy, or watching Conner do things exactly like his daddy, make my breath catch in my chest. I have to smile and nod when I want to hide; to laugh out loud when I want to cry; to take Conner places and do things with him when I want to stay locked away.

When is it going to seem real, to seem normal to not have Mike here? When am I ever going to be okay? When will our son be okay?

In a little over two months, it will be three years since Mike passed. I can't imagine the emptiness we feel lessening. Difficulties continue to plague us. But even amidst this lies gratitude.

I am grateful for my family and friends. I don't know where we would be or what we would do without them. They have listened when I needed to cry, they have helped with Conner when I have attended meetings and other work things, they have helped me with housework and have helped me run the farm, and they have tried to comfort me during my terrible moments.

But none of them are Mike. They cannot bring him, or our life with him, back. They cannot fill our smiles with genuine happiness. They cannot know the secret fears that run through our minds daily. They cannot take away the fear, sadness, anger, shock and confusion. They stand alongside my boy and me, and they do their best to keep us from falling completely.

Widows have it rough, but their children have it worse. The worst pain is not being able to "fix" it for our children. I would, and I know every other widowed parent out there would, give anything to bring peace to my child's broken heart.

Everyone keeps telling me, "In time things will get better."

I call bullcrap.

Time has not healed us. Time has not magically made things better. Time sometimes is a ticking time bomb, teasing me with an explosion of emotions. Sometimes I catch myself stopping in the middle of everyday tasks. I stop and look around for a few seconds, shaking my head to awaken my thoughts to reality. This is it. I'm doing this alone. Conner is growing up without a father. How weird and how tragic is that?

Conner began writing letters to his dad on some of his very worst days. I have read the letters and they make my breath catch in my chest. I have read them aloud to Mike. I have placed the letters in our safe deposit box and I sometimes visit the bank just to read them. Conner does not know I do this.

I cannot come to terms with the fact that our baby boy has to write letters to his dad, letters he will never receive an answer to. It takes such bravery to write the letters, knowing he will never get to send them. Conner's strength is astounding and he doesn't even know it. Conner writes them like Mike is still here.

One day I felt Mike sending me another letter from Heaven to Conner.

> Dear Conner,
> Hey buddy, it's Dad again. I got your letters. Your mom read them to me. Thank you for writing them. I wish I could be there, son. My gosh, it is crazy how this happened. How our worlds changed in one quick second. I'm sorry that my leaving hurt you and Momma so much. I sure didn't mean for it to. I never meant to hurt you guys and to leave like I did.
>
> But you know what God told me when I got here?
>
> He said, "Son, welcome home. It's time to rest. I've got everything taken care of for you here and you don't have to worry and work so hard anymore. Come see your family that you've missed so many years and rest."
>
> I looked at God, Conner, and my first question back to Him was, "What about my family, God? What about my boys? My sons are so young and Conner is only ten years old. This isn't fair on him, God."
>
> And you know what He told me back, Bubba?
>
> He wrapped his arm around my shoulders, and as we started walking toward the sunlight I could see shining across the way, He said, in almost a whisper, "Mike, I promise you something right now. I have your family wrapped in My Grace. I am with your family and I will see them through every day and every night they have to live without you. I will listen to every cry and every prayer and every fear and every dream. I will listen as they beg Me to bring you back, but I will send them little reassurances that you are okay with Me. I will listen as they get angry with Me for taking you, and I will send your wife the right words to

tell your son, Conner, when he asks why you had to leave so soon. I will know when their hearts are breaking all over again, I can feel them shaking all the way up here, and I will send them your song to help them breathe easy again. I will watch as they learn new routines and go to new places, trying to fill their sadness with something new and exciting, and I will send them the happiest memories of you to help them smile. When their tears fall on their pillows as they cry and they feel like they can't go anymore without you, I will move them closer to each other in the night. When doubts flood their minds about the future, I will give them the idea that you would want them to be okay without you and that you understand they have to do what they have to do. Trust me, Michael, you are my son, and I love you, and would never leave your family."

It took me a minute to wrap my mind around it, but I knew I had to. So, I did. I turned to look over my shoulder for one last time, wondering if I could still see my little brown-haired, brown-eyed boy in the distance. But I couldn't. God told me He wanted me to wait a little while before He would let me see you.

But when I finally did, it was AMAZING! All I could do was smile!

You are growing so tall, son! You're going to pass your brother pretty soon. I know he hates that, but boy, it's gonna happen!

I saw you write the note to your friend the day you asked her to be your girlfriend. You were trying to be pretty slick like your ole dad, huh? Good job, Bubba.

But I want to tell you that I saw your note the next day, too. When you woke up the next morning, crying to Momma that you were scared to have a girlfriend because Daddy wasn't there to give you advice. I asked God to send Momma the words she needed. I'm so glad it worked.

You have a very smart mom, son. She's smarter than I was about most things. Farming, no, but she's learning. She's doing a good job learning all the stuff I did before I left. You remember that and listen to her.

I'm so glad she talked you through it and you kept that pretty little girl as your girlfriend. I felt proud of you after that talk . . . when you decided to keep your girlfriend and listen to your mom's advice. You became more of a man in that moment, son. You doubted yourself. You became weak for a minute because you didn't think you could do something on your own. But you know what? You went ahead and had the courage to keep doing what you were doing. You listened to your mom tell you she could handle those girls . . . and she's right. She knows what girls need to hear. She knows how you need to treat them. Trust her. I did.

So, when I started seeing and hearing you, it was so cool! I watch you at school and, man, how cool is it that you're in Beta! I know you're going to do that drawing contest and I want you to draw one of those cool work trucks like we used to draw. I bet you'll win something! But even if you don't, I'll love it anyway. And everybody else will, too.

I've been seeing you make new friends at school, too. That's good. You guys do some pretty funny stuff at school. I like when you guys play football, and it's cool how sometimes you talk with your friends and you sound just like me.

You know what else I saw the other day?

I saw a young man, dressed to kill, in a pair of dark Levi's and boots, take his momma's hand and walk with her to the dance floor at a wedding. I saw a little boy forget his troubles for a minute and wrap his arm around his mom's waist and slow dance with her, and my gosh, I never had more pride swell out of my chest than I did right then. Your momma took my breath away fourteen years ago, and let me tell you, son, she took it away again that night. She looked so beautiful to me. She was the prettiest girl there. And you were the best-looking guy in the whole place.

I watched you both slow dance to two songs. You did so good, son. You made your momma feel like the luckiest woman in the world. Because she has you and you are a part of me and her put together. You got all the good stuff out of both of us, you know?

Her smarts when it comes to reading and writing; you're so creative with your stories.

My artistic side with all of your drawings of trucks, jeeps, and deer. You sure can draw.

Her heart. You sure got her heart. It's so big I don't know how it keeps from bursting.

My sense of humor. Mom doesn't always appreciate it, but we sure do, huh?

We are both so proud of you, Conner.

I wish I could be with you to tell you all of this in person. One day we will be together again, and you know what it will be like? Like we never were apart. I promise. You won't even know I've been gone. We'll laugh, and hug, and kiss, and jump for joy. I won't know all that I've missed, and will miss in all the years to come.

Do you know why? Because I see it all. I WILL be with you when you kiss your first girl. I WILL be with you when you walk into high school as a freshman. I WILL be with you when you go to the Junior Prom. I WILL be with you when you graduate high school. I WILL be with you when the first girl really and truly breaks your heart in two. I WILL be with you when you beg somebody to fix it and heal it, and I'll sure do my best to reach down and comfort you. I WILL be with you when you fall in love for the first time and know she is the one. I WILL be with you when you ask her to be your wife, and I WILL be with you when you meet her at the end of the aisle. I WILL be with you when you buy your first house and when you have your first baby. I WILL be with you when you watch your children grow.

Conner, I WILL be with you every day of your life. Even if it's not in the way you wish . . . I'm here. I've always been here, and I always will be. I'm not going anywhere. Sometimes it might feel like I'm not there, and sometimes it might be hard to know I'm there, but all you need to do is remember.

Remember the times I held you when you were a newborn and danced with you in the living room, singing you songs so low so Momma couldn't hear. Remember the times we rode around in the truck on the farm, just telling stories and laughing. Remember all the times we went hunting for deer and how excited and proud I felt when you shot one. Remember all the days we sat on the computer looking for toys at Walmart.com or at old Scouts and Jeeps on the internet. Remember all the times we sat in my office, me working at my computer and you "working" . . . a.k.a. drawing and making a mess, right beside me. Remember all the wrestling matches and special nights we had on the floor. Remember all the birthdays and Christmases and Fourth of July parties we had. Remember how much fun we always had. Remember my laugh. Remember my hugs and kisses. And when you do, I'll be there. I'll come to you in memories that warm your heart. I'm always there, son. Always.

So, for now, I've got to go again. Grandpa Bob wants me to tell him more stories about you. He's sure proud of you, too.

I need a couple more favors, okay?

I need you to tell your brother how proud I am of him. Tell him I watch him at college and he's doing well. Tell him I miss him with every ounce of my being and it's amazing to watch him grow into a man. He's so good looking and smart and funny. Tell him I sure miss his crazy stories he always tells. I miss his laugh. Tell him to keep going to school and working hard. Tell him I love him.

I need to you to tell your mom a few things, too. Tell her she is still beautiful. Tell her I am so proud of her for her new job. She sure is a hardworking woman. Tell her I see how worried she is, and how heartbroken she still is, but that God is making her a little stronger every day. Tell her she's doing amazing with you, and the bills, and the farm, and all of it. Tell her that it's okay to want to be happy again.

I want her to go out again someday and laugh and flirt and be made to feel beautiful again. She deserves that. She's never going to try and replace me, son, you have to know that. But Momma needs to feel loved and safe and wanted and needed. You won't understand that until you're a grownup. Momma and I talked about what would happen if one of us passed away way before it happened. We both told each other we would want the other one to find someone new. Mom will pick good. She picked me, right? So, trust her.

Don't fight her when she decides to date again. And I know Momma . . . she won't even think about dating until she's good and ready! And she'll make sure it's all good before she even brings you anywhere near someone else. But when she does, be nice to him. Make me proud. He's not going to try and replace me any more than Momma is going to. He will know the story behind us. Mom will tell him on the first date. He'll know all about me and our life and the love we share. And he'll understand. If he doesn't, then you know your mom won't keep him around. So, make me proud and be nice, okay?

It will eventually get easier and it'll be really cool to have another person who loves you and wants to hang out with you and have fun. That's what your mom was for your brother—another person to love him and want to be with him. She never once tried to replace his mom or be his "new mom." It will all work out buddy, I promise. Give it time and be patient.

Tell her I love her and support her in everything she's doing. I'm so proud of how she is making it work every day. She's way stronger than she thinks she is.

I love you more than words, Conner Luin. Take care of yourself and your mom. Tell your brother how much I love him, too. Be nice to your friends. And CLEAN YOUR ROOM, please! Your mom is getting so mad about that!

Keep working hard at school and doing your best. I'll talk to you soon, Bubba. Keep my letters coming because I love to read them.

Sweet dreams little man. I love you forever . . .

Dad

Chapter Twenty-Five

HAVE YOU EVER FELT GOD TALKING TO YOU? FELT ON YOUR heart words you *know* He would say if He stood in front of you? Many times over the past three years I have felt God's presence on my heart. One particular time, it was like a conversation I would have with an old friend. After all, that is how we are supposed to feel God, right?

"Okay, enough of this crap. You can do this and you're going to have to quit wrapping yourself in sadness! Focus! Snap out of it! You have a son to live for and he is more precious than anything or anyone else! Go and have fun with him! Quit lying around the house in your pajamas every chance you get. Get up and get dressed. Smile! LAUGH! Go and be with friends! DO things! Mike would. If you think he would have sat in that house for over a year, you are kidding yourself. I mean, seriously . . . you knew your husband better than anyone else. You guys even had this conversation before dating again. You know he would. Number one, he could not have done all his jobs and raise your son alone. Number two, he would not enjoy being alone. It depressed him when he was alone before you. So, you're done just sitting there! GET UP! LIVE for crying out loud! Just because you live that does not mean you don't still love and miss Mike. It doesn't mean you are a bad person or a bad widow. It does not mean you will not think of him anymore, or that you have to stop wearing your wedding ring, or his flannel shirts to bed. Mike will always be your husband; that's how he left this world. But child, it's okay to breathe and let yourself be open to new beginnings. I promise I have you. I have Conner. You guys are so important to Me and I'll never forsake you or lead your heart in a wrong direction. It's okay. Life is going to HAVE TO move forward. No, I didn't say you'll have to 'get over it' because that will never come. But you CAN 'get ON with it' . . . and that means LIFE! Get on with life because I promise you it's too short not to. I love you, child, so trust me. I'm the one talking to you and telling you it's okay to move forward even if it's in teeny tiny steps. Remember your conversation with Mike on your first date? 'I need to take baby steps, like seriously, because I've never dated anyone before. I married my high school sweetheart, so I've only known being with him. I'm not sure what you expect, but I need to take baby steps.' The two of you were in love in a week. Take baby steps, my daughter. But step back into life with your son strong by your side. You two go have adventures and make memories. I love you."

Right then I decided life was only going to be what I was willing to make it. No one is going to turn my life into some shining storybook for me. I have to do it. I have to decide to follow God's path for my life. I have to listen when He tells me to stop being so lame!

What I want widows (well, everyone) to know is that *finally* seeing the light is a completely valid feeling of widowhood as well. And it's okay to want to be happy again!

I will always be a widow, no matter what life brings down the road. I will always be Mike's wife, but it will be okay with him if I eventually become someone else's wife too. Mike will understand, and he will be proud of me. He and God will send me someone who will be good for both our son and me.

So, life must begin anew for those of us in the throes of grief. No matter how difficult it is for us to accept our reality post-loss, it is our reality nonetheless. After all, I have this, and God has me. I can't go wrong.

And since grief is a cold-hearted witch, even with knowing God has me and will never forsake me, sometimes I still feel like all that I am is never enough without Mike.

I was always enough for Mike. I was beautiful enough, sexy enough, smart enough, and funny enough. I was a great cook, a wonderful homemaker, and a fun partner. I worked hard enough, I listened closely enough, and I fought fairly enough to make him want to stay.

I was always enough.

I absolutely detest that all that I am now is not what I was before.

I do not take care of myself like I should. I don't feel beautiful; I feel fat and gross. The confidence Mike gave me has diminished. I lost quite a bit of weight after his passing, but now I "eat my feelings" so the weight has come back on.

I don't feel sexy. I burned my sexy underwear and nighties when Mike died. I packed them up in a box, marched down to our trash burn hole, and set the box on fire.

Sometimes I fear that I might be alone forever. I wonder if the other millions of widows across the world felt this way only in the beginning, or if the insecurities last forever. Even if they move forward, fall in love again, maybe remarry . . . I wonder if these thoughts, like mine, will always be ingrained into a widow's brain? How unfair is that to the new man?

So, I don't know if I will ever meet someone new; I want to . . . I want to flirt and laugh and find enjoyment in someone and dress sexy and all that. But I am a widow, a mom, a sister, a daughter, an aunt, a friend, an educator, an aspiring writer, a child of God, and a struggling woman. That's a whole lot to take on.

I don't want anyone's sympathy. When I meet a new guy, I worry he only wants to date me because he feels sorry for me.

I don't want their empathy either, because I don't want anyone to "understand and share" my feelings. I would not wish this understanding of my feelings of despair upon my worst enemy. Empathy places oneself in another person's world. It is a terrible world in which widows and children of widows live, one plagued by everlasting grief. I hate the feelings associated with widowhood and wish it did not exist. I wish no one would ever have to experience the depths of grief so many of us know.

But here is what I want for me and for my son:

I want others to be patient with us. We don't always arrive where or when we say we will; sometimes the grief gets the better of us and we cannot make it. I cannot count how many times we have rejected invitations to dinner, parties, or other events. Sometimes my little boy cannot make it to class because of the anxiety that invades his wonderful, bright, and beautiful little boy mind. I hope others are patient with him, even more so than with me.

Grief takes time, and it does not ask anyone for their opinion. Sometimes we have good days, maybe a lot of good days in a row. Then we are thrown into the pit of our darkest memories of when Mike was taken and when we put him in the ground, and we cannot function.

We are not pretending; we are not crying or acting sick to get out of anything; it is real. Grief does not come for a little while and then go forever; it comes and goes, comes and goes, and comes and goes.

Sometimes we need others to step back and give us space. Don't expect too much togetherness with us. We often need to be alone with each other to process the memories of the loss we have endured. We don't always need to be around others when we are wrestling with our memories.

This one is a tough one though, because sometimes we want you to come closer and wrap your arms around us. Let us fall to the floor in sobs; fall with us and hold us there. Hold us tighter when our screams get louder. If you fall with us and hold us and let us cry, others will know it's not a circus show; it is a pain like no other and we need pure, unadulterated love.

We want people to look at us like we are normal. No one looks at us the same anymore; expressions of wonder, fear, and sympathy are what we get now. From everyone. Everywhere. Every day.

Look at us the same as you used to. Yes, we are different. Yes, we have changed in more ways than you know, but we are the same, too. I am the same Roni who loves music, dancing, laughing, and her family. And Conner is the same boy who loves hunting, fishing, guns, the military, and his family. Remember, even in the midst of this tragedy, pieces of us remain intact; they might be difficult to spot to the naked eye, but looking at us like we are ogres crossing the street makes us feel awkward. I dart my eyes to the ground to avoid the looks.

We want you to listen to us. Sometimes we need to talk about Mike at the most inconvenient times. I have called my sister at ten p.m. because I couldn't breathe. I needed to cry and tell her for the millionth time that I don't understand, that I can't believe he is really gone. Even years later, I still need to call my sister and say those words.

So, listen to us when we need to talk about Mike. He was our world and we miss him, but we love hearing his name and sharing stories about him. I have risen from restaurant tables and had to make a speedy exit because my breaths were coming in gasps and the tears were unstoppable after telling our story to our friends. It is good for us to talk about our story. We hope it will help others.

We often want people to remain quiet. Telling us, "Well, it must have happened for a reason," or "He's in a better place now," is not cool. I will never know the reason, because God does not intend for me to know. Keep your reasoning to yourself for my husband being ripped from my grips, my son's father/hero/best friend being torn from his hands, my mother-in-law's firstborn gone in a heartbeat.

We don't need to hear that he is in a better place. There is no better place for Mike than here with his family. We know people do not mean any harm in saying those things, but please don't.

More than anything, we want you to pray for us. Pray for our strength to keep breathing; for our will to keep living. Pray for our patience and acceptance in times when they both seem the most fleeting; for our ability to forgive stupidity and rudeness. Pray for our faith to only increase; for us to get out from under the financial burden left upon my shoulders, and to get out from under it in a positive way. Pray for us to one day have less anger. Anger toward Mike for leaving even though he didn't mean to, anger toward God for taking him, anger toward those who have told lies about us for no other purpose than pure malicious intent. Pray for us to one day be free of any guilt we feel for our "what ifs" and "should haves" with Mike.

As often as asked, I will stand on a stage, whether that is a church altar, a crowded women's conference, or a stage at a widow's retreat, and tell our story. I want to help someone. I want them to know that what they are experiencing can be survived. I want to be the person who helps someone not to give up hope. Not to give up faith. Not to give up life.

The truth is, no one has it right. No one does widowhood right. No one does grief right. We each do it the best we can and try to make it through the day. My biggest fear of doing something wrong is with my son. I wish I could give him back his childhood and his daddy. I wish I could be the kind of mom I used to be: happy again, silly again, cry less, laugh more, and have the energy to leave this house.

Losing Mike has brought my own mortality to the forefront of my mind and to my little boy's mind. Conner can't help but fear that I will die suddenly, like his dad. He cannot stand to be away from me for very long, and even when he is, he is constantly texting me, "I love you." Don't get me wrong, I absolutely love his messages. But I hate that he has so much fear in his little boy mind that he sends them out of that fear. His anxiety has increased over the past few months. He is seeing our school counselor weekly and is still on medication.

So how can you convince your child that you will be okay? Your spouse wasn't sick . . . you aren't sick. Your spouse was careful . . .

you are careful. But it's irrelevant. God is the only One who knows when, where, how, and why. I might be able to accept that, but I can't figure out how to help an eleven-year-old accept it. That totally unexpected, shocking, and devastating phone call changed my son's and my stepson's lives forever. And we would give anything to have Mike back.

We miss Mike so much, and we love him just the same. The boys are growing and working hard to make a normal day out of their grief, but I know it riddles their minds as much as it riddles mine. I am proud of them both.

We wish our family was whole again. Back to our perfectly imperfect life that we loved so much.

Mike's death drew a definitive line in our lives: *before Mike* and *after Mike*. My little boy has suffered depression and PTSD. He is not the same boy he was before. I'm not the same mom I was before. Why does it have to be *clearly* evident that there is an "old" Conner and Roni and a "new" Conner and Roni?

Since Mike's death, I have often wanted to run away. I have wanted to throw in the towel and remove myself, to not be here in the same place as before. I have wanted to leave this house flooded with Mike and infinite reminders of our tragic loss. I have wanted to sell. Pack up and move. Start fresh. Loss is devastating. Grief is debilitating. Life in the state of depression/anxiety is crippling. And people on the outside don't understand.

I wish I had the financial and emotional stability to homeschool my son and travel the world. To fill his childhood with as many wonderful memories as I possibly can, because he has been robbed of so much. I wish I could buy a huge RV (the big bus kind), buy a homeschool curriculum, pack the RV full of everything we need, and place the gearshift in drive.

Here, I am sad. I am afraid. I am lonely. I am miserable most days. And so is Conner.

We pray. We keep breathing. We hope. But we are constantly reminded of the absence of happiness in every photo, every piece of furniture, every nook and cranny of this house and farm.

He has never seen our Tahoe, and he would have loved it. He has never sat on our new sofa, and he would have napped on it daily. He has never seen me as a school principal and he would be proud.

And because of all of this, some days *just suck*. And on those days, I can barely function. I don't want to talk to people, and I don't have energy.

We lost our world. Conner and I live crippled in fear and grief and insecurities. Fear invades the grieving heart. It is grief's best friend. A widow experiences fear of the present and a fear of the future. She fears that she will never emerge from the depths of grief. She fears that she will never be able to stand on her own, to rear her child on her own, or to laugh without forcing it.

We are trying to navigate this new life without maps or compasses. Thank God, He is in control and not us. But one day maybe the fear will subside. Unfortunately, I have no time table on when the fear will leave me or leave my son.

Conner did not just lose a dad, he also lost me. The real me. The "before" me. Conner has two overpowering fears. One, that I will die, and the other, that I already have died and he's never going to get me back.

Wow. Look at what grief has the power to do. Change us. Kill a part of us. But with that death, it also creates a new us.

Before Mike left, I enjoyed sitting on the front porch with my husband beside me. We would listen to the crickets and whippoorwills sing. We would hear the frogs bellow and the cows chomping grass. We would talk about our days, our dreams, our plans together. Front porch sitting had a positive connotation.

Now, after losing Mike, I often sit on the front porch with all the familiar sounds dancing around me. Crickets chirp their familiar songs, heifers' call to their babies, hummingbirds buzz by the rose of Sharon bushes, and the breeze tickles my skin. It is quite beautiful. Yet I have felt miserable. I think I could still enjoy the sounds and the feeling of the cool evening air, just not *these* sounds and *this* cool evening air. They are different. Tainted. They used to be Mike's and my sounds and evening air. Now they are dark and sad and angry and lonely. The sounds don't bring me joy; they increase my sorrow.

During my front porch sitting I ponder my parenting skills; my widowhood badge that I wish I could return; my judgment. Hell, even my sanity.

I am scared. I am scared of failure. I am scared of failing at being a solo mom; at being a good principal; at being a good friend/sister/daughter/aunt. I'm scared of being alone forever. I'm scared of being okay again and forgetting the sound of my husband's voice. I'm scared my son's anger toward me is only going to build over the years. I'm scared he's going to turn on me. I'm scared people are going to look at me with pitiful gazes if I stay here. I'm scared to move away but I'm scared to stay.

I'm scared that from here on out, no matter who I'm, with or where I am, or when it is . . . front porch sitting is forever tainted. I'm scared that *I* am forever tainted. I fear that no one will ever want me or love me the way Mike did.

At about sixteen months into widowhood, I decided to have a conversation with Conner about me dating. It was awkward, this conversation I never dreamed I would have with my son. I wanted to tell him that I'm ready to meet someone to have fun with. I crave love. I crave companionship and laughter. I crave someone to share my life with.

I wanted to be the one to write the story of my life, exactly how I wanted it written. I didn't get that; it's not my job to write the story of my life. The deck is dealt by the Lord. There are things I wanted that I didn't get, and things I want that I'm afraid I'll never have.

I wanted to be the one to grow old beside a man who loves me endlessly. I wanted to be the one to straighten his tie the day our son becomes a husband. I wanted to be the one who holds hands with the love of her life as we walk through the hospital doors to greet our first grandchild.

I wanted to be the one who rests beside him in our king-sized bed every night for the rest of our lives. I wanted to be the one who laughs until I cry at his silly stories. I wanted to be the one who matters most when everyone is watching or when no one is. I wanted to wake up next to him every morning.

I wanted to be the one forever.

I'm so scared I'll never get what I want now. I'm confused as to where and how and even when I may completely move forward and away from the crippling grip of grief. I want to be loved endlessly again. I want a manly man who will not shy away from me when we are out and will place his hand on the small of my back. I want a man who will worship the ground upon which I walk.

I want a man who will share his fears and secrets with me, and will protect mine when I share them with him. I want a man who will sweep me off my feet and tell me I'm beautiful, even though I'm not. I want a man who doesn't have to be prompted to compliment me, whether it be for my looks, cooking skills, parenting skills, or whatever.

I want a man who will surprise me with pizza and beer. I want a man who will make me weak in the knees with just one kiss. I want a man who will accept, appreciate, and love my flaws and fears and insecurities. I want a man who will be my son's friend, but who will also help make sure he becomes a good man. That's one hell of an order to fill, and it won't be easy.

I want a man who will respect my son's space and time for healing as well as mine. Conner has suffered a terrible loss, one from which he will never fully recover. I want a man who will recognize that and will love Conner through it. I want a man who will never try to replace Mike in Conner's or my eyes.

I will not try to replace Mike. I will not try to find a new Mike. I will not look for Mike's traits in a new love. That is unfair, and I will not do it. Instead, I will give all the new me to a new man and I will love without fail. I will offer my entire heart and being to the right man, and he will understand that our love does not take the place of Mike's and my love. He will not be jealous of Mike. He will support Conner and me and will help us celebrate Mike on our special days, like Mike's birthday and the anniversary of Mike's death.

We both have room for another love, but the man I want will have to recognize that it's another love and that our original love for Michael will never go away. It will not be lessened. It will not be replaced. The widowed heart only grows after loss. It makes room for so much more love because it was robbed of so much. The widowed heart needs love and happiness. Love becomes sacred to us. We cherish it. We value it. We crave real love. We crave happiness.

Dear Michael,
    I've no control over the tears that fall while I write today. I am in absolute denial today as I have been every day for the past year.

    I thought this vast emptiness inside the depths of my soul would be filled with new memories made with our son this year. I thought maybe I could genuinely smile and laugh and begin to live again. But each new memory still has a tinge of sadness because you're not here. And my laughs and smiles have not been genuine, but rather forced, and oftentimes faked.

    I'm still not angry with you, even though you broke your promises to love me forever and to grow old with me. You promised to sit on our front porch and watch our grandkids play in the front yard one day. You promised to want me forever; to kiss me every day, and to hold me close when I needed you to. I wish I could have you back. I felt safe and loved and wanted and needed because of you. Now I feel scared and vulnerable and weak and lonely because of your absence.

    They say time is supposed to heal everything, but this first year has offered no healing. I am forever burdened with sounds and images of that day. It's like someone has taken a brand and permanently scarred me with the details of that day, and of the days between your leaving and your funeral. It's as though they happen all over again each new day and I'm so tired from them. I'm writing this at three a.m. I can never sleep without taking a sleep aide. I dream of you and of December 29, 2014, and of January 1, 2015. Conner had it right last year when he said that December 29, when we lost you, marked the worst day of his life, and that January 1, when we lowered you into the cold ground and said our final goodbyes, marked the hardest.

I fear that I'll never learn to love again. Part of me never wants to, because it's almost as if I feel that by loving someone else I'll be cheating on you . . . on us. I fear that I'll maybe start to like someone but will be too scared to really like him because he is not you. And no one but a widow understands this feeling. I know of widows who have moved on to dating someone within a few short months of her husband passing, but I couldn't do that. It's not that I am judging those widows who move on quickly, but I'm judging myself and my own lack of strength. It would be nice sometimes to laugh and flirt with someone, to go out to dinner and watch a movie, or to a ballgame. But everything I did for thirteen years was surrounded by you. How am I supposed to do these things with someone new when I've done them all with you, and I'm not ready to let you go? It's so scary.

But dating again isn't as scary as raising our son alone. What if I screw up somehow? What if I haven't taken him to enough counseling? What if my punishments are too harsh? What if they aren't harsh enough? What if I've coddled him too much since losing you? What if I start dating someone again and Conner doesn't like him? I don't want to permanently screw up our kid. But I guess it will be what it will be, and I will keep trying to do my best. I pray to God to protect our boy and to keep him safe, healthy, and happy every day. I pray strength over him so he can grow into a fine young man who is kind, hardworking, generous, loving, affectionate, passionate, smart, gentle, and humble.

Some days I want to take a sleeping bag and a pillow and never leave your side. I just want to exist there and maybe fall asleep with my hand on your tombstone, so it's almost as if I'm resting my hand on your chest like I used to.

I often find myself calling my sister for a break down. I know it makes her own grief worse because of my breakdowns, but I feel I have no one else to call. Many friends offer, and that is amazing and wonderful, but I do not want to burden my friends. I know it is a heavy load for my sister to bear and she has carried it for the past year. She has sacrificed sleep and peace to listen to me sob endlessly into the phone.

Everyone in our family misses you. You were such a strong spirit. You had such strong character and beliefs, and even though you sometimes forced them onto people who didn't want to accept them willingly, no one can deny that you had purpose. Every day you had purpose, and even if we didn't always agree to your methods, we all revered you because of it.

Because of your purpose, drive, and work ethic, I decided to create a scholarship to honor you. I have been thinking about it for a while, and decided with the upcoming mark of one year without you, I would dive in feet first. I posted it in the newspaper; had your boss post with all MRWA communications; and had Amy share it on Facebook. I opened an account at the bank for family and friends to donate to and created a scholarship application form to give to both our county schools. I talked with your mom about helping select winners and I think she was greatly honored. I hope to honor the scholarships for as long as I live, and maybe Conner will take it over when I'm gone. I hope you are proud of me for trying to keep your legacy alive.

I can't believe you're gone and it is so surreal for me to say out loud that I've been alone for a full year. The longest I had ever been alone before you left was between my divorce and our beginning, which was only a few short months. I haven't been held or kissed, or had someone whisper he loves me.

Chapter Twenty-Six

Many realizations occur to us widows after a few months as members of the crappiest club ever. One such realization is that there is no escaping grief.

If I go anywhere, the memories flood my mind. For thirteen years, I did everything with him. Ballparks, shopping malls, restaurants, recreation parks . . . regardless of where or who I am with, my mind wanders to those memories. I imagine that unless I move across the country, I'll never have a place without memories. And at this moment, I've no intention of ever leaving our home.

And I'll never have Mike to help with parenting. I need him to talk through fears, sicknesses, stitches, school work, and everything in between. We made decisions together and together we would all sit at the kitchen table for homework time. I did the English and Reading, Social Studies, and usually Science, and Mike handled the Math. We worked as a team on organizing Conner's folder and backpack, on signing parent documents, and so on. From here on out it'll just be me. So, we search YouTube often for tutoring.

I'm trying desperately to build a life for Conner and me, but it's just not happening. It's not coming together. I keep realizing what I'll never have again, what Conner will never have again, and I cannot get a grip on it. I cannot force it deep down inside enough to ignore it and move forward. Sure, I have moments of what everyone else calls "strength," but they seem to be lessening lately. I don't know why; I guess it's just the continuing cycle of grief. The one I'll repeat over and over and over again until I get to see my husband.

My mind never shuts off. I am overwhelmed by sad thoughts unless I'm busy at work. That is the way of the widow.

Do you realize how many widows or widowers are in your town? I never really thought about it until I became one, and in my little bitty town there are several; some are younger than me, some are older. And then I think, what about those parents? Those step-parents, siblings, friends, and so on who are grieving their loss as well. When someone dies, an entire community of people is affected.

So, my train of thought wanders toward what a widow/widower is thinking. Here is usually how my thoughts travel:

I wake up and think of Mike and his absence. Every single morning, the absence of Mike is my first thought. Wow . . . is this real? Is he really gone?

And then it goes straight to the day it happened. The phone calls, the crying, the difficulty breathing, our son kneeling in the gravel screaming. I think about Mike being alone at the concrete plant and I curse myself for not having gone that day. Maybe I could have helped him or saved him. We had almost surprised him with lunch.

Then I think about going to where it happened. I have almost pulled down that road whenever I pass it, but I usually have Conner with me and I will not take him. But I think I need to go there, almost like it's a sacred place where I'll be able to feel him. It's the place where he took his last breath. I think I need to go there just once.

Then I think "what is wrong with me?" Am I ever going to be okay? Am I ever going to wake up and all is right with my life? Is my son ever going to be okay? And then anger sets in.

I am angry that we have been dealt this hand. I want to fold and get an entirely new deck, not just a new hand. And then I grow mad at Mike a little bit. I become mad at him for not listening to me all the times I begged him to slow down, to sell something, to downsize.

And then my anger turns to exhaustion. This thought process could happen in a matter of seconds, almost in unison, or drag out for an hour or longer. Regardless, it is utterly exhausting.

I always have these great plans of working out in the morning, thus breaking my routine of sitting in my chair with a cup of coffee and staring at his picture. But I don't. Because I am tired, a tired I cannot explain. My body feels like it weighs a thousand pounds, my heart will beat out of control, I shake when the thoughts get so huge, and I'm so physically, mentally, and emotionally drained that I set my alarm for one hour and forty-five minutes before I have to leave my house. I only need twenty of those minutes needed to apply my makeup and style my hair. It takes me that long just to process my life and my thoughts.

To spare others, I fake it. I slap on a smile and laugh and give off energetic vibes so I can run my building well. But inside, I think about how broken I feel. How I wish he could see and be proud of me; but also think how if he were still here, I would probably not be a principal or we'd never see each other.

But I hide it from the world and from everyone I love and then when I need a release, I let it out in sobs. Sometimes that happens in the shower, but sometimes my poor son has to watch his mom fall apart in the car.

I miss my old life, my husband, my family being whole, true laughter, genuine smiles, holding his hand, kissing his face, the wrinkles around his eyes, his calloused and worn hands, his snoring, his warmth next to me, his mischievous grin, his surprises, his raspy voice, his compliments, his texts and calls, his label on my phone "Love of My Life," his confidence, his walk, his jokes to me that he liked the wiggle in my walk, his time he spent sitting on the couch with me in the mornings, our cups of coffee together, his drive, riding in the middle of the seat so close to him in his truck, the sound of the diesel engine roaring up the hill when he came home, cooking him dinner, his compliments on my food, the way he would come up behind me while I was getting ready in the bathroom and put his arms around my waist and tell me how much he loved me, his morning hugs . . . everything.

I pay attention to statements on social media that I shouldn't.

"Happiness is a choice. We get to choose whether we are happy or not." I recently read this statement on someone's Twitter feed and felt a desire to vomit. And cuss.

Really?

Let's think about this. Maybe I'm just extra wound up and angry because my husband died. I have so much to say about this whole "happiness is a choice" line of crap. I did not *choose* to become a widow and a solo parent at thirty-six. I did not *choose* for my ten-year-old son (now twelve) or my seventeen-year-old stepson (now nineteen) to lose their dad.

Happiness is a choice? *How?* When tragedy of this magnitude occurs, we don't have a choice in our emotions or in our lives. Emotions take control. Grief is a process, a cyclical up-and-down road through which we travel half the time with blinders on. We don't know how to navigate grief. Grief does not include happiness. Loss does *not* include happiness. We did not choose the loss; therefore, how in the world can we *choose* happiness in a time like this?

Let me tell you what else I *do not* choose:

I do not choose to awaken to silence.

I do not choose to roll over in hopes of seeing my husband beside me, but instead seeing an empty space (except on nights Conner sleeps in our bed).

I do not choose to carry knots in the pit of my stomach.

I do not choose to feel a massive lump in my throat that I force to stay put or else the flood comes and rips me apart.

I do not choose to pay these bills alone.

I do not choose to feel like a failure as a parent when I'm questioning my own parenting tactics, or how to answer a question Conner has.

I do not choose to be the only name on our son's report card and school documents.

I do not choose to mark "widow" on the stack of school forms, or to write "deceased" on the father section.

I do not choose to shake uncontrollably when I get really upset thinking about it all.

I do not choose to experience random spastic moments where I just cry and freak out about my fears and my insecurities.

I do not choose to have a heart that begins racing at random and inconvenient moments.

I do not choose a mind and heart that now don't work like they used to.

I do not choose this mindset of not planning for anything beyond an hour or two in advance. What's the point? I had my whole life planned and look where that got me?

I do not choose to feel sad.

I do not choose to feel angry.

I do not choose to suffer from depression.

I do not choose to feel more uncertain than I ever have before.

I do not choose to receive looks of pity.

I do not choose the feeling of defeat.

I do not choose loneliness in a room full of people.

I do not choose this life of widowhood. I do not *choose* to *not* be happy.

I do not have a choice.

I did not get a say. I was not asked if I was ready for my husband to die. I was not asked if I would rather he die now or later. I was not asked if I'd like to raise my son alone. I was not asked if I wanted to bury my husband in a beautiful cemetery on a freezing cold January day.

I cannot flip the switch and turn off grief. I did not choose a visit from death. I cannot just ignore that the love of my life has been gone almost twenty months and I'm starting to freak out about the approaching holidays and two-year mark.

I wish to God that I could choose.

Now some of you may be thinking, *well, lady . . . God gave us free will so yes you* do *have a choice! You* do *have a choice to be happy!*

Here is what I have a choice in:

I choose to be grateful for what I have and what I had.

I choose to be me, and if my grief and my crazy widow brain makes you uncomfortable, then you need to depart from my life. Because in the grief process, I do *not* have a choice.

I choose to breathe deeply when the anxiety rears its ugly head, making me want to crawl into a hole and hide from everyone and everything except my son.

I choose to pray for strength, and for everyone I know and love, every single day.

I choose to try and live my life the best I can under the circumstances.

I choose to pray for others who are less fortunate than me, in any way.

I choose to love my friends and text back when I'm feeling "normal" and to not text back when I'm sad.

I choose to fight every day to get out of bed and put one foot in front of the other.

I choose to laugh with my baby boy when we feel like laughing, and I choose to cry with him when we feel like crying.

I choose to reach out and help every single widow that I can!

So, don't expect me to believe that I *can* choose happiness. I wish it more than anything. If I did have a choice, I promise you that the angels would be jealous, because Mike would be sitting beside me, his fingers intertwined with mine, and our son would be playing joyfully. All would be well and I would be happy.

    I'm trying. I'm trying to bring little pieces of happiness back into life, but for the love of God, I'll *never* understand or choose to be happy in widowhood.

    But I will choose to heal.

Early morning cups of coffee,
sitting one love across from the other.
Feet touching on the edges of the couches
where they meet in the corner.
Moments of conversation and sideways grins
while sips of warm black liquid are taken.
A hand reaching over to touch the other
ever so gently and warmly.
A cute giggle out of such a burly
man when something funny is said.

Whispers into the pillow late at night
while the rest of the world sleeps.
Moments of silence between two souls who
look deep into the other's eyes.
Understanding of a love like no other when
not one word needs to be spoken.
Youth fading into middle-age, wrinkles and
extra pounds coming.
But loving just as much as the day they first met
over a phone call on an October evening.

Date nights spent staring into each other's eyes
as much as the teenagers around them.
Midnight snuggles on cold winter nights
when they should be sleeping.

Long talks of dreams and plans as cows graze
in the fields below and the trees dance.
Plans and hopes and promises made to withstand
the tests of time.
A head gently tilted to rest on a strong shoulder
that makes her feel safe every day.

They were in love.
She was safe.
They had each other.
Her son had a daddy.
Her heart had its other half.
Life was complete.
The world was as it should be.

It's a Different World . . .

Early morning cups of coffee taken alone
while she stares at his picture and flag on the mantle.
Feet curled in under the blanket while she feels
cold in the loneliness of her home.
Silence remains, and speaks stronger than any
giggle or conversation they used to share.
Her hand is alone, empty of his, her wedding ring
changed sizes and fingers, but on the same hand.
A tear instead of a giggle, at the memory of
something funny he used to say.

Whispers into the pillow late at night,
begging for peace and mercy from God.
Her eyes stay closed as she squeezes them tight
trying to block out the pain that keeps her awake.
She knows there will never be a love
like theirs was.

Her youth is fading and she feels more aged,
more wrinkled, and weary and heavy-laden.
And she loves him still, as much as she did
on that phone call one October evening.

Date nights are now her and their son,
watching dads and kids and trying not to.
Midnight wakings because she dreams of him,
when she should be sleeping.
She doesn't talk about dreams anymore,
knowing it will do her no good.
She is afraid to have any kind of hopes or dreams;
she can't let go of the old ones.
She misses his shoulder to lean on, she misses
feeling safe and protected.

She is still in love with a ghost.
She doesn't feel safe anymore.
She has no one who understands.
No one to talk to.
Laugh with.
Love with.
Hold on to.
Promise the world to.
Her son struggles daily.
And she can't fix it.
She can't take it all back.
She can't carry it alone.
But she has to.
So she prays.
and she prays . . .
and she prays . . .
And she is grateful.
Grateful to friends.

To family.
But she is still alone.
At the end of the day.
When she climbs into bed.
When she picks up the phone to dial.
She is alone.
Her other half is gone.
Her best friend is gone.
Her knight in shining armor is gone.
And so is her heart.

Chapter Twenty-Seven

THE MORNING FINALLY ARRIVED WHEN I AWOKE FOR THE 365th day as a widow, and it felt as if I had only been widowed a day. I realized that I had spent the year feeling sad, lonely, and broken. I relive that fateful day which took so much from me, every morning when I wake and every night when I close my eyes.

I wrapped my arms around my husband for the very last time on December 29, 2014. I kissed him good morning and told him how much I loved him as I buried myself into the warmth of his flannel shirt. His arms were closed around me like they always were, as he kissed me and said he loved me back.

We stood at the kitchen sink and embraced. I felt the stubble of his whiskers and took in the scent of his skin. I heard his raspy voice that could calm me during any storm. For the last time, I looked into his hazel eyes that melted me.

Tragedy shook my soul like it never had. It took a piece of my little boy's innocence and robbed him of a normal childhood. Tragedy robbed me of pure, untainted happiness and security. I will never get that again because my heart will never regain its full composure.

As I fell to the gravel, in utter terror and disbelief, screaming out, I didn't have time to think of the most appropriate way to tell our son that his daddy was gone forever. I just blurted out, "Conner, your dad is gone, Bubba . . . He had an accident at work and he's gone."

I watched my child fall to the gravel beside me with tears streaming down his innocent face. I helped him walk back to the house, where he stopped and vomited outside our door. None of it seemed real to me then, and it doesn't seem real to me now.

I wrote about the one year mark of Mike's death. I placed this particular journal into a sealed envelope and placed it in the safe deposit box. It reads:

> Every day seems like the day when I reached across the bed and felt for his presence, feeling the rise and fall of his chest. It seems like yesterday when I fell asleep to the music of his snoring. It seems like yesterday that I was laughing, living, and loving like I had nothing to lose. Then one day I lost my rock. I lost the desire to laugh . . . to live like I did before . . . and to love anyone besides him.
>
> What now?
>
> It has been one full year and I don't know what comes next. I wish it were a magically healing date that once a widow reaches the one-year mark, she is then set free from grief. I wish that the one-year mark released all widows and fatherless children of all pain, loneliness, guilt, regret, fear, insecurity, shock, and disbelief. Maybe a shield of armor should then be presented that reads, "Wonder Widow: Warrior of Loss."
>
> Instead, that one-year mark brings back the vivid details of the worst day of my life. It brings with it more fear to top off the already mountainous list of fears I have. The day brings guilt for being a non-present mom some days over this past year. For instance, when I spend too long sitting in the recliner, not getting dressed, and not being a good mom. There's regret of not going to surprise my husband with lunch when it happened; maybe I could have helped him if I'd been there when he fell.
>
> The day also brings insecurities, uncertainty of my son's and my future, the pang of the shock and disbelief that still makes my breath catch in my chest.

And this day adds the cherry on top of a mountain of pain and loneliness. Not just for me, but for every person who knew and loved my husband. His mom will relive those horrible details, but she will also go back to Mike's childhood and remember the tiny baby boy she held in her arms. Mike's sister and brother will relive childhood memories and will replay their own regrets and sorrows.

My family will not only remember the loss of Mike, but also the loss of my happiness. They will remember the sight of my tear-stained face, the text or phone call to tell them of the terrible tragedy, the way I couldn't breathe for crying so hard, or how I could not walk through my own house alone those first days.

They will remember my little boy and his immense strength that first day and in the days following. They will remember how he helped me calm down each time I broke. They will remember the people who poured into our home and brought food, drinks, and anything else they thought would be helpful. They will remember Mike and all of our Christmases, Thanksgivings, and birthdays. They will remember happier days.

And the boys . . . what will they remember? It will be the same as everyone else: flashes of the day he left us and of the day we placed him in the ground. They will remember their favorite memories of playing on the floor with their daddy, of wrestling and special nights in the living room, of sitting in his office talking for hours, of riding around on the farm and "helping" Daddy. They will remember chocolate milk in a sippy cup and picking up sticks to roast hot dogs in the field. They will remember playing catch in the yard and family vacations to Orlando, to Branson, and our camping trips.

But they will also think of what memories they won't be able to create. And that will be the most difficult. The boys will think of the absence of their dad at their weddings, at the birth of their first child. They will think of the times they would love to have their dad present to help them choose a new vehicle, or to pick a good rod and reel. They will feel the absence of their father every step of the way. And I cannot do anything to take that away. I pray God wraps the boys in His Graces today, tighter than He has ever wrapped them. I pray the boys find strength in each other and in me.

And as for me, I will remember random things, such as surprises of pizza and beer; sticky notes trailing to the bedroom; flowers on my desk after our first date; opening our first Christmas gifts to each other while sitting on his bed; falling in love under the stars while we stopped in the middle of the field and held hands in the old 'Yota.

I will remember working with him on the farm; picking up walnuts with him and the boys around the machine shed; the summers we spent before we were married; me traveling around the state with him for work. I will remember our silly engagement story; the day we learned we were pregnant with Conner. I will remember the mischievous smile that crossed his face when I waited for him, dressed up for date night; and the last date we had weeks before he passed. I will remember how we stayed beside each other through our toughest struggles.

My memories will come like the floodwaters that rush the creeks and rivers of Missouri today.

I will rely on my faith and on my family and friends, and on my widow sisters I have met along this journey.

Two days after that one year mark, I spent my first widowed New Year's in hell, my own personal hell from which I imagined there was no escape. I could not awaken from what I wish were a dream. It was real, terrible, tragic, and shocking. And it still continues.

I have spent more than one thousand sleepless nights in our king-sized bed, awakening to the reality of my life every morning. I have spent more than one thousand days reliving the nightmare. I have spent more than one thousand days missing my husband.

With all those days and nights, like a baby taking her first steps, I have begun to step toward hope. I have finally begun to plan for a future.

Don't get me wrong, the grief is still a part of me. It has built its home inside my heart and will always have a place to rest. It will take its turns acting like an unwelcome guest who takes charge and overrules all order.

But, with the grief now lives my desire to plan and hope toward happiness and healing. I cannot attain these goals overnight. I cannot attain them within the next year. Maybe not even within the next five years. There is no timetable to grief.

In the meantime, I will work toward my plans and I will remain grateful. I plan to rise from the ashes of this personal hell. I plan to continue breathing and doing my best to survive the days, to survive the financial mess my husband left me with, to work hard at being a single parent to our son. I plan to continue working to be the best person I know how to be, to love my family as hard as they have loved me, to continue writing in hopes of encouraging other widows.

I plan to heal.

And I plan also to remain grateful. Grateful that by walking through hell I have learned, grown, loved, and been loved. Success. Even in my sorrow and grief, I have managed to remain grateful for what I have, for what I had, and for the amazing friends I have made, both at work and via the crappy club of Widowhood.

I am grateful that I have survived without asking for anything from anyone. I am grateful that through this year, I have learned not to take any crap from anyone. I am grateful that through this year my son and I continue to survive. I am grateful that my relationships with my family have become stronger. I am grateful for the many offers from family and friends, such as staying the night so we aren't alone, cleaning if I need it, cooking if I need it, and so on.

I am also grateful that God has carried us through the first three years. He has never forsaken us. He has listened to our many prayers. He may have taken my husband away before I was ready, but He has still given me a healthy son. He has allowed me to continue being Conner's mom. He has let me take on different roles in my career, and he has allowed the words to continue pouring onto my pages. He has made me strong. He will bring us happiness again someday.

So, even though 2015, 2016, and 2017 have been pure Hell, I plan to prosper in the years ahead. I have been to the bottom of the pit, so the only place to go now is up, right?

I have cried myself to sleep too many times to count and have offered up infinite prayers to take the pain and loneliness away. I have held our little boy close to me as he has wailed for the loss of his best friend, his hero.

I have lost sleep. I have worked on this farm, and in my career, to keep things going for me and our son. I have moved cows, fed cows, worked cows, mowed fences, sprayed fences, and much more. I have learned to drive a tractor, to bush hog parts of the farm, to learn what I need to do in order to be self-sufficient.

I have paid my husband's debts, and learned way too many things about probate court, estates, and lawyers. I have also learned things about people I once thought I could trust. People I thought cared about me and my son.

I have learned that my husband did not fulfill his promises to me to make sure all paperwork—from insurance beneficiaries to title work on property—was handled correctly for our children. I have learned he kept much of the debt blind to me.

For a time, I learned to be alone in my grief. I lost my desire to go out and see people and do things with anyone other than my son. When we are not in school, you'll usually find us holed up in this house. I'm not as extroverted as I used to be.

I also lost my desire to talk. I text way more often than I talk with anyone. I often ignore calls, not because I don't care about the person calling, but because I haven't the energy to lie, and fake it, and pretend we are doing well. If people really heard the truth when they ask, "How are you doing?" they would never call again and would probably fall into a dark depression themselves.

Widows hate that question. I want to respond with, "Well, let's see . . . my husband died, so I'm just freaking peachy." Seriously. Don't ask that question.

When Mike left, I lost my best friend, my right-hand man, my wingman. I lost my favorite voice, my softest kiss, and my imperfectly perfect love.

I lost me.

A part of me will never return, because it died with him. The Roni who walked proudly into a room with her husband beside her is gone. She is weaker, more vulnerable, less sure, less happy. She is broken into a million pieces, shattered against the shock of losing her husband. She is in a darker place; and even though she smiles and laughs, there is and will always be a tinge of pain.

The Roni who married Mike no longer exists. I liked her. She was happy. She was secure. She loved and was loved deeply. She felt safe and comfortable. Life was not always sunshine and roses, but it was theirs.

It's difficult to stay positive. One day I feel a strand of hope, and the next I'm at a bottomless pit of anguish. That's how grief works.

But it's okay. Because God has this. God has us.

It's a struggle staying the course. It's a struggle to keep it together and not throw up my hands and run away. It's a struggle not to fall into the trap of vicious rumors that seem to plague all widows. Rumors of affairs, of flagrant financial spending, of going "off the deep end."

But I won't veer off course. I won't run away. I won't fall into the trap of evil.

I still love my husband. More than words.

Dear Michael,

Life was never perfect. But it was ours. We made amazing memories through our time together that haunt me every single day.

Remember when we spray painted the old International camouflage? We had CCR playing in the background and a six-pack of beer. We laughed a lot and had the best time.

Or what about the time the longhorn cow knocked your hat off while you were giving them range cubes and I couldn't get out of the stupid Scout? I was scared to death you would walk back to me with blood all over you, but luckily she didn't even bruise you.

Remember the first night when we rode around the farm in the old 'Yota? You told me later that you knew then and there I was the one meant for you. You told me you loved that I was a country girl, a tomboy; that I was beautiful but simple enough that my hair could fly all over the place with the windows down and I didn't care.

Remember how much I tried to impress you when we went gigging together for the first time? I wanted to show off and I kicked your butt at gigging. I learned very soon that you probably let me because you were an amazing gigger. You were amazing at everything you did.

Remember when we were checking that crazy group of cows you bought off someone and I was on the back of the four wheeler with you when one came running and almost kicked me? I grabbed onto you so tightly and you gunned it, almost knocking me off the four wheeler!

I remember the first time you took me to meet your mom and Gayle. And the first time you took me to the forty acres. We sat on the four wheeler and talked right in the middle of a hollow in the woods.

I rode with you all over the state during the summer just to be with you. I met lots of people and you smiled so proudly when you introduced me to someone. I had never been made to feel as good as you made me feel.

I remember you coming to my fourth graders' Christmas concert in my first year of teaching and the day you surprised me while I stood on recess duty. You came walking across the playground and I couldn't believe I had found someone who loved me as much as you did.

And what about the first Christmas as we opened gifts to each other on our bed? You got me a necklace and a few other small things, and I got you Carhartt jeans in the wrong size! The waist and length numbers were exactly backward! But you laughed and were okay with it.

Our first two years were spent learning about each other, falling in love enough to figure out how to get over the screaming fights we sometimes had, and building a life we could be proud of.

When we got married I felt so happy. I wanted my family there, but it was okay that they weren't because it meant more time for me and you. You looked so handsome in your black suit from JC Penney, and I looked so young in my ninety-nine dollar David's Bridal dress.

We married at seven p.m. on August 9, 2003. We laughed through the ceremony at the short stature and dramatic effects of the lady who married us, and then changed into comfy clothes for dinner out. We were so exhausted after the day that we went straight to sleep after dinner and went home first thing next morning.

When we met our son on May 17 of that year, I was the happiest woman in the world. What more could I want? I had the man of my dreams who held my hand and said, "Push baby, push!" My final dream for my life had come true. I was holding in my arms the tiniest, most perfect bundle of the best parts of me and you.

We were a family.

Besides making it through the good times, we made it through the hard ones too.

We often struggled financially. We struggled with time and the lack thereof. We fought over my feelings being hurt too easily, and you not caring about what I wanted you to care about. We struggled with infertility after we had Conner. We fought over where to live and what land you wanted to buy. We fought over how many vehicles you had, half of which never ran. You were a jealous man and we fought about that. You hated when I was singing in a band with the boys and you would never tell me, "good show," but you would tell others. You drank too much and we fought about that, too.

But I would do it all over again, Mike. In a split second. You have to know that. There is not one part of you I don't miss, even your bullheaded, jerk side!

Baby, I can't believe you're gone.

I can't believe I'm spending our twelfth wedding anniversary talking to a stone, sunken to my knees with my shoulders shaking as I sob.

I don't know how to wrap my mind around the fact that you have gone. I don't know how to accept it fully and start moving on. Some days I smile and laugh and don't even cry. Others I relive every grueling detail of the day you died. I want you back so bad.

I don't know how to do this on my own, babe. Conner is pushing every boundary he can and I'm so tired. I don't know how to make anything better or easier. I don't know how to handle all the money problems and debt over my head. I don't know how to deal with the lawyers, court dates, probate, and accountants. But besides all that, I don't know how to be okay without you.

I haven't taken a breath or made a single move for thirteen years that didn't revolve around you.

I look at your Marine Corps picture and the neatly folded flag in the flag case that rests upon our fireplace mantle and I stare at it in disbelief.

I walk into your office, which looks almost exactly the same. I put your flannel shirt on in the evenings when it finally cools enough to wear it. I open your drawer in the bathroom and run my hand over your razor.

I'm so incredibly broken.

I miss being happy and in love. I miss being wanted and needed and finally appreciated after all these years. I miss the rasp in your voice and your phone calls and a million texts a day. I miss that you won't get to grow old with me on this front deck like you promised you would. I miss the dreams of us watching our grandchildren run around in the front yard.

I want to run to you and wrap my arms around you so badly. I want to hear you say my name and that you love me. I want to do nothing but sit and hold your hand. I want to go on date nights and scoot to the middle of the truck while I tease you with kisses as you drive. I want to feed cows with you and have you teach me to drive the tractor again every hay season. I want to make a dozen bologna sandwiches for your summertime farm hands. I want to pick up your dirty laundry and shake out the cow manure and clay mud from your jeans. I want to sweep up the crumbs from under your spot at the kitchen table. I want to cook your favorite meal, steak and potatoes. I want to smile when those texts arrive or when I see "Love of My Life" on the screen, since that's how you are programmed into my phone. I want to laugh with you and take in all of you.

I don't want to deal with all life brings at me on my own. Gigging and deer seasons are right around the corner and I thought about them the other night while looking at deer in the field with Conner. I don't want to ask others to take us because you aren't here to do it. I don't want to ride the fences during deer season to make sure no one trespasses. But that's exactly what I'll do.

I'll do it because of our little boy. I'll survive against my own will that sometimes tells me to melt away into nothingness. I'll work my tail off at my new job to make you proud.

I'll raise our boy as best as I can. I'll continue wiping my tears as they flow uncontrollably some days. I'll smile at new people I meet even though I want to hide from them all. I'll continue to nod and then lower my head trying to avoid eye contact every time someone in town looks at me. I'll continue to ignore their stares of pity. I'll drive your truck on days I really miss you. I'll sit in your office chair when I pay our bills. I'll do this and so much more because I have to. Because God wants me to.

I can't die today. I can't meet you in Heaven until God sends me your way.

So, I will look for you in the sunrises and sunsets. I will watch you grace our farm through the fog that rolls in the evenings. I will touch my cheek gently when you whisper to me in the fall breeze. I will see your eyes twinkle in the sparkle of the first snow of every winter. I'll think of you every time the rains fall and our road floods, thinking of how hard you worked to clean up the mess it always left behind. I will smile with sweetness every day the sun shines down on my skin.

I will forever think of you and of our life; some days those memories will bring me the only peace I know. Other days those memories will break my soul into a million pieces and bring me to my knees. But I will continue to rise every day . . . to breathe in deeply . . . to survive my loss.

I love you, Michael Richard. I hope I feel you today as I remember our wedding day and how much we love each other. I miss all of you, since having you as my husband was what made me whole.

Until I see you again . . . I'll keep loving you.

So I ask, what now? I don't know. No one knows. But life will unfold just as God has planned it, and one day I hope to genuinely smile and laugh and live and love without any pain attached.

I hope to relive only happy memories, and visits to the cemetery will become less agonizing.

I hope our son grows into an amazing man.

I hope my heart, and the hearts of everyone who knew and loved Mike, find peace.

From the ashes of hell, I am ready to rise.

Stronger and wiser.

We held a memorial shoot for Mike at our farm just months after his passing. My friend Amanda Sly with Dazzle Photography took them. It was important for us to include Mike's truck. He loved that truck and I drive it still as often as I can. Conner began wearing Mike's and my dad's dogtags soon after we lost Mike. We found one dog tag in Mike's desk and my dad offered Conner one of his. He still wears them both to this day.

To the New Widow

Chapter Twenty-Eight

Hope is often linked with having faith in the unseen and unknown. Hope has been said to be the anchor to our soul.

Grief handicaps its victims; it robs us of our initial hopes for a happy life. Eventually, new hope grows where the scars of the former hope remain. New hope intermingles with the old hope and through this connection, growth occurs.

We grow.

Hope grows.

Life begins to grow again within us and around us.

More than one thousand days ago, I became a widow.

My husband was ripped from my life in the blink of an eye. On that day, I spoke words to my son that broke me: "Your dad is gone, Conner. There was an accident at the concrete plant and your dad is dead."

I needed help to make it from the recliner to the bathroom during those first few days. My limbs would stop working and I would break into terrible, draining sobs.

I couldn't drive myself for days. For months, yes *months*, I walked in a fog. I could not process Mike's death. I functioned on survival mode.

The feelings return whenever I go back to the first text from that terrible day.

My breaths become labored when I look back to see him on that cold metal table, his body covered in a white sheet. His left arm exposed so I might hold the hand of the man I had loved for so many years.

Not one single detail of my husband's passing have I forgotten. Not one detail has faded.

When I began writing, four months after Mike's passing, tears stained the keyboard. With every stroke, my life poured onto the pages in front of me so that I could get it all out. I wrote with purpose: release the pain from within, or it would to kill me.

The words before you come from the different stages of my journey through grief. I have spent three years enveloped in darkness, fear, worry, and shock.

In the beginning, there was no hope. But, God spoke to me over and over.

God spoke to my heart amidst all the cemetery visits. He whispered love and hope and promise to a broken and shattered soul. He brushed my cheek with the gentle breezes of fall and spring, the seasons my husband and I spent so much time together. He caressed my heart when the depression left me aching.

I am forever grateful to a God who gives hope. And I am forever grateful that through the pain, He sent me my purpose.

My purpose has become so much bigger than myself or than my sorrow. Have I done it all right? Absolutely not. No one does. Am I perfect and healed? Most definitely not.

Do I still crumble to my knees and curse the day Mike died? Unequivocally, yes.

Do I believe with all my heart that it will get better for us? Unmistakably, yes.

I promise that one day, not immediately, and not fast enough to satisfy your broken life, you *will* climb from the abyss of pain and loss and suffering and guilt.

You have to *fight!* You must!

You must claw your way out . . . kick and scream and fight to get to the other side. Because *no one else* can, or will, do it for you. You will be bruised and tattered, exhausted, and scared. But you *will* survive this, despite what your heart and soul sometimes scream at you.

You will break down, no matter if three years or twenty years pass. You will still cry, but not every day. You will still miss your other half; your soul mate. But eventually, against all odds, you will begin to recognize that life does go on. Life does move forward. We do not "move on" from a loss so devastating. We instead move *forward,* forging a new path for our own healing. We take the love we shared with us every step of the way.

Three years ago, I did not think there would ever be happiness in my world again, and quite frankly, I did not want it. Not that I contemplated suicide, but I did not want life to go on without Mike in it. My heart could not fathom that a life without Mike could exist. The realization that life *does* go on, did not sit well with me and it pissed me off when people told me it did.

The widowed community is one of such love and acceptance. We make connections and lifelong relationships because we *get it*. I have had new widows reach out to me over the years, seeking advice, wanting a shoulder to cry on, or just needing an affirmation that they are not in fact losing their mind.

I will always listen to another widowed person. I will always pray with them. I will always wrap my arms around them. I will cry, scream, or pray with them. I will send them scriptures when they seek comfort. I will do whatever I can to help every widowed person know: better days are coming. Just lean into God.

Dear wister,

I know how insanely scared and in shock you are. I know that you can't believe the world has just crashed down around you. I am so sorry.

Sweet wister, your home will soon be filled with lots of people. It is going to be overwhelming in so many ways:

overwhelming love and gratitude for all the people who care enough to show up; overwhelming sadness for the reason they are in your home; overwhelming denial, shock, and hurt because now that your home is overflowing with people you love, the most important person is missing.

You're going to have to breathe. Just keep breathing. Say a prayer for strength.

I know your hands are shaking and your heart is beating uncontrollably, yet in the same instance you fear it will stop beating. It won't stop. It will beat to a new rhythm one day. It will take a while. I know you are sitting in a chair or on the couch and you cannot grasp that this is the new reality.

Sweet wister, I'm incredibly, unimaginably sorry. I truly am.

Your first few days will feel like they are going to break you in half. You will feel moments of numbness to everyone and everything around you. It will be surreal and your soul will not accept the reality of your spouse's death. It is a strange realm, an out of body experience, where you stand from afar watching yourself crumble to a million pieces.

When you see your love for the first time after that last breath has been taken, you're going to have to muster the strength to face the empty shell. I chose not to see Mike's face. He took a hard hit to the side of his face and head when he fell into the concrete mixer. I did not want to see him any other way than as his handsome, perfect self. But I did want to hold his hand.

You do what you're comfortable with, and the funeral director will be more than willing to oblige. Don't be afraid to hold his hand. Don't be afraid to lay your head on his chest. You will miss the sound of his heartbeat that used to be there when your head rested on him. I know you will fall down, but someone will be there to pick you up. Don't worry about it. Fall if you need to. Scream if you need to. Pray if you need to.

When you visit the funeral home to make arrangements, lean on those close to you. Don't go alone and don't be afraid to go slow. Your thoughts will be sporadic; it will help to have family there. It will be ridiculously difficult to choose your spouse's final resting place. Don't go crazy expensive. What's the point? Your spouse cares not what he or she goes into. You will know when the right one appears. Mike's was an old barn-wood casket with an image of a hayfield embroidered on the inside. It was him.

You'll know. And when you know, it will bring you to your knees because it is real.

In the beginning, sleep will not come without medication. You will have dreams. Some will be of sweet memories, some will be of being with him again, and some will be the reality of how he died; all will be heart breaking and gut wrenching. You will awaken with tears streaming down your face. Your hands will shake uncontrollably and you'll hyperventilate. Take your time to get your breath back. Just hang on tight, my dear wister.

The first morning after will be the strangest morning of your life. The old habits that the two of you shared will be hard to break. You'll roll over in anticipation of seeing him lying there, but instead there's an empty space that seems to stretch a mile. Your heart will break into a million pieces all over again. It's going to do that for a long, long time, my wister. And I'm so sorry.

You'll rise to an empty and silent room and will relive the day you lost him. You will have to re-accept your new reality every single day for a long time. You're going to need help. It's going to make you angry that you need help, but do not let your anger or pride get in your way. Accept the help. It shows how much you're loved.

If you have children, know they will probably be stronger than you in the beginning. You will have so many friends and family around that you won't have to worry if your children are being fed or played with. They are. They are distracted for the first while. Children are resilient. In the beginning, their strength will surprise you, but only because they are in shock. Grief will grab hold of them sooner or later, and it will kill a piece of you.

Hold them tightly, take them to counseling, enlist their school counselor to help, and if need be, ask your doctor about medication. It took me a long while to move past the stigma of my son being on an anti-depressant; but if it is what he needs to help him fight the suffering, then we will do it for as long as necessary.

We are grown-ups. We can mask much of our pain and suffering. We can grit our teeth, clench our jaw, scream every cuss word ever invented, get up, shower, and slap a sickeningly fake smile on our faces. Our beautiful, innocent children who have been robbed of one of their parents haven't mastered the art of faking it yet. Hold on tight. Pray hard for strength.

After the dust has settled, the funeral has passed, and the people are gone, that is when things get real. Ugly, scary, messy, and so much more. You are not the only one to go through this. Reach out to others who have experienced this similar devastation. We all love each other instantly and feel a familial connection with the first point of contact.

I fell apart so many times the first several months. The first few weeks, I experienced my first of many panic attacks. When you do, have someone fetch you a cold damp washcloth and close your eyes and will your breaths to slow. It's going to take work, but you will come back. Just hold on. Those panic attacks are scary and terrible. Mine hit mostly out of anger or shock that my husband was suddenly dead, and my family for which I had prayed my entire life was gone, no longer complete.

There is a whole community of us, my dear wister. We are in every town and city. We are in every school district and mall. We cover the walls of Facebook, Twitter, and Instagram. We blog to get both the ugliness and hope out. Lean on us. Make connections. Read, listen, write, and speak. Speak your pain and your truth in the struggle to survive widowhood. Tell your story so that some other unsuspecting person can know that when it happens to him or her, it is normal to have the roller coaster emotions and thoughts.

You're not going to go crazy.

You're not going to die.

Your children will grow into strong adults.

You will forge new paths and you will come out the other side much wiser than you ever imagined.

You will learn to not plan long-term and that is a gift. Do what makes you happy, when it makes you happy!

If work sucks, then quit! Get a different job.

You will learn to live for the moment with your family and friends.

You will call them more, text more, visit more, and never part without saying, "I love you."

You will break down into uncontrollable sobs at the most inconvenient times, but who cares? NOBODY.

You will lose weight in the beginning but eventually your appetite will return.

You will be so incredibly tired that you can't muster the energy to exercise (unless you already had that habit fully developed).

You will hear new meanings in certain songs.

You will find there are some songs you can no longer listen to, and some movies you can no longer watch.

But you will find new music and new movies.

You will laugh again. And I mean that true side-splitting laugh. I know it seems impossible but I promise, you will.

You will live again, my sweet wister. It will take a long time; it will be a difficult struggle.

You will fall down many times but keep praying even when you feel angry.

Keep praying even when you think you don't deserve anything good because of all the cussing you've done.

Keep praying for strength. He won't disappoint.

I know with all my Christian heart that God has a plan. I believe that one hundred percent, but that belief and knowledge will not do one ounce of good the first little while. I have to be honest: it won't. It won't bring you comfort. It won't settle your fears or calm your churning stomach and shaking hands. It won't prevent your soul from imploding because you miss your spouse so much. It won't stop your tears from falling for a million hours or your child's heart from being ripped out; it won't help you sleep at night or understand why. It won't.

I was so weak in the beginning days and weeks; I had to be helped to walk almost everywhere I went. I couldn't drive myself anywhere; I slept during the day when I could, because night brought new sadness. I would reach across to feel Conner beside me and cry because he was where his daddy should be.

I didn't wear makeup for months after Mike passed. It took me weeks to get back to work full time, and I was more timid and quiet and sad. My students were understanding; they gave me quiet when I needed it. I left my classroom to sob in my principal's office several times. Reach out to your boss and coworkers. They are human too. Let them help you through the days.

I am weaker in some ways; I feel like my voice is weaker. I don't talk as much or as loudly as I used to. I don't go out with friends often, and I'm not as extroverted as I once was. I haven't grown all the way back together, and I never will. I'll be scarred and bruised from this tragedy for the rest of my life and so will you. But, one day . . . and it will take a long time; eventually, that weakness will give way to strength. I promise it will.

I'm so terribly sorry, my sweet wister. I hate more than anything that anyone else has to experience what I have experienced. Plain and simple, no sugar coating, it is a screwed-up lifestyle to live. And worse—we didn't choose it. We don't want to live the lifestyle of a widow!

I'll never understand why my child had to fall to his knees beside me in our gravel drive that cold December day. I'll never understand why, after my life was finally what I had hoped and longed for my whole life, in the blink of an eye it was all washed away. I'll never understand the ache that is and will always remain in my soul.

But keep praying. Even when I'm angry with God, I never stop praying. I don't understand why we lost Mike. The world lost a good, hardworking, handsome, and smart as heck man that day. We lost out. God gained.

Widowhood changes you. It changes where your mind wanders. Widowhood changes your perspective, your attitude, your speech, your fears . . . it changes all of you. In some ways, you will be weaker, too. But strength will come in the right moments.

When weeks or months have passed and you clean out his drawers, strength will come. Strength will come when you go through the closet and fold his clothes nice and neat for the last time. Strength will come when you decide to either donate his clothing to Goodwill or save them for your son, if you have one. Strength will come when you look at his face in the pictures on your walls and you whisper, "I love and miss you."

When months, or a year, or more than a year has passed and you decide to date again . . . strength will come. When you take that first phone call or text asking if you'd like to go to dinner sometime, strength will come. Strength will come when you get dressed up for another man other than your husband. It will come when your hands are shaking with nerves and your stomach is doing flips, but you get dressed, do your makeup and fix your hair anyway.

Strength will come when you look in the mirror and see such sadness and brokenness in your own eyes but want so desperately to live again. It will come when you walk out to him and he smiles and says, "How are you?" Strength will come when your nerves settle enough to laugh when he says something funny. Strength will come when you find yourself having a good time and the guilt sneaks in.

Do not feel guilt! You did not choose to be a widow, and you are doing nothing wrong by going on a date. Nothing. You are not cheating, but people will talk about you anyway, so take that step in strength. Take that step back into life. It's totally fine if nothing comes of it . . . but it is equally fine if you find yourself falling in love again.

Strength will come when you decide to go on a second date, and it will come as you smile when you see his name across your phone screen with a text just saying "Hi." Strength will come when after a date you come home to see your husband's picture on the wall, and you still tell him you love and miss him. That's okay!

If the man you decide to date cannot accept and appreciate that you still love your husband, then he isn't worth having. If he is the right kind of man, he will know there is no competition with a dead man; there is just an endless love. You were in love when he died; you had no say in the end of your marriage and still love him. You always will, but you have enough love inside of that beautiful beating heart of yours to love your husband and someone new. It's a different kind of love and a different kind of relationship, but both are beautiful.

Strength will come when you visit your husband's headstone and tell him about this new man. You will sob on your knees while you talk to him and tell him about it. But it will be strength that brings those words to fruition. It will be scary and you'll be nervous to tell him, but it will be good for your soul.

He wants you to be happy. He wants you to step forward, for you and for your children. He would do the same thing, and he is proud of you for taking that step. And what is so strange but beautifully wonderful, is when you know it is the right guy, you will feel your husband smiling and nodding his head that it's good.

When you find yourself laughing a genuine laugh, strength will come. You'll find that strength is with you when you go to bed without crying, or when you wake with a smile on your face because you realize you're surviving what you thought would kill you. Strength will come when you feel happiness again.

Strength will come from those countless prayers you have sent up, even in anger. It will come when you have to stand and walk to the casket before he is lowered into the ground. Strength will come when you sleep in your bed alone for the first time. It will come when you visit the local grocery store and make it out without breaking down.

Strength will come when you fall to your knees to pray with your child who is so broken. Strength will come when you have to speak to different people about bills and what is owed and who is the beneficiary on life insurance policies. Strength will come when you return to work, even if it is only for a couple of hours at first.

When you decide to go to church, strength will come. It won't be easy because you will be washed with so many emotions, but go. I'm not saying you must go all the time, but go. Somewhere . . . sometime . . . go. Pray for strength, and thank God for what strength you've been blessed with thus far.

Strength will come in so many ways and in so many things that you do and say, my sweet wister. I know exactly how you felt in the beginning, and you might still be in the beginning. And you might think I'm full of it!

I know, that's exactly what I thought when I read the "widow books." (Too many of them are self-help . . . well, seriously, you can barely breathe so you don't want to read a bunch of self-help crap), but just keep breathing and praying for strength and I promise, it will come.

But this is not a "self-help" book—this is an honest experience from a young widow who thought her life was over the day her husband died. That's all. Just widow-to-widow talk about my experience in this crappy club.

Wister, no one will understand the thoughts and demons we fight, not unless they became part of our club, and none of us would ever wish this upon anyone.

I miss him. More than my family can understand. More than my friends and co-workers can understand. More than even I can understand at times.

Life moves forward, but no one realizes how truly difficult it is to accept that truth.

I can no longer be angry about life's continuing cycle. I can no longer be afraid to breathe new life. I cannot, and will not, give up on everything I have ever enjoyed and loved just because my husband died.

I will now, forever, and always times infinity love and miss my husband Mike, and the life and love we made together.

But I promise that I will survive and live my life to the fullest!

I will laugh until I cry.
I will love someone else as much as I love Mike.
I will dance to my favorite songs.
I will sing to the top of my lungs.
I will giggle until my sides hurts.
I will smile a true smile.
I will raise my son to be a good man and to follow God.
I will pray to thank God every day for bringing me this far.
And I promise . . . you will too.

I can say that I love you because I do. I love you because we are sisters even though we never wanted to be. I'll help love you through this hell if you need me to; we all will.

Just keep breathing.
And pray for strength.
God will not forsake you. He will not leave you. His love will guide you home. And so will the love of your husband.

Much love and prayers,
Your wister,
Roni

I am now, forever, and always times infinity . . . still his.

Acknowledgements

To my little boy, words cannot express how proud I am of you. You held me up those first few days with the strength of a million men, and I cannot even begin to describe how proud that made your daddy also. I would give anything for this not to have happened, but your resilience and growth from this tragedy will prove phenomenal one day. Rely on God, just like mama told you the day your daddy went to meet Him. Pray every day. Never cease in your love for Christ, in your love for your mama, or in your pursuit to become a good man. We both love you endlessly and I know that one day, you will change the world. You are such a blessing and I am your biggest fan. This book is for you. MTW.

To both boys, your dad loved you and loves you still, bigger than the sky.

To my editor, Karen, and to everyone at WiDo Publishing, thank you for believing in me and in my story. Thank you for your patience and diligence in making this book something magical for which I hope my son will be proud.

To my family, Mike's family, my friends and widowed family, thank you for loving us through it. Without your help, your support, and your love, I could not have made it. You have made Mike proud.

To Michael, when you stole my heart all those years ago, I never knew you were going to leave me way too soon. None of us were ready to let you go. But, the Lord knew you were tired and that you needed rest. Thank you for the two boys you brought into my life and for building a family with me. Thank you for all the tiny ways you surprised me over the years; no one would have ever guessed you were such a romantic, but I knew, and was so lucky to have you. I hold in my heart the knowledge that every day the sun is shining on your handsome face, the beautiful green grass is cool beneath your feet, your smile is lighting up the entire sky, and you are happy. We miss you more than words can ever say, and my heart aches for a love like we had. Until we meet again, I'll be loving you, now, forever, and always times infinity, your wife.

And finally, I owe all my thanks to God. I have fallen from Grace more times than I can count, but He has been right there with His hands to pull me back up every single time. Without my faith in the Lord, there is no telling how this journey through tragedy and grief would have turned out. Thank you for fighting for me, Lord; I am unworthy, but forever blessed.

"The light shines in the darkness and the darkness has not overcome it." —John 1:5.

This is for Conner, so that he may forever hold his parents' love in his hands. So that his children will one day turn the tattered pages to find a love worthy of a million lifetimes. So that one day, Mike's grandchildren may come to know how cool of a guy their grandpa really was.

Conner, I hope that you know how much your dad and I love you. Thank you for holding my hand through it all and helping me heal. You are my world and every single page, every single word, every single ounce of this book is for you. I love you. MTW.

About the Author

Roni Hollis is a small-town teacher whose world changed entirely when she became widowed in December of 2014. She and her son, Conner, live on their farm in Missouri.

Roni began writing and serving others in the widowed and faith communities just four short months after losing her husband of eleven years. Her drive to turn her pain into a purpose has seen success in the blogging world and has reached many widows and widowers across the United States and beyond.

Roni's desire behind her poignant memoir is to tell her story of love, loss, and hope in order to help others find validation and peace in their journey with grief.

CPSIA information can be obtained
at www.ICGtesting.com
Printed in the USA
LVOW12s2008181217
560205LV00001B/106/P